W9-BFZ-723

Emergency Planning for Maximum Protection

Emergency Planning for Maximum Protection

Richard Gigliotti
Ronald Jason

Butterworth–Heinemann

Boston   London   Singapore   Sydney   Toronto   Wellington

Copyright © 1991 by Butterworth–Heinemann, a division of Reed Publishing (USA) Inc. All rights reserved.

No part of this publication may be reproduced, stored in a retrieval system, or transmitted, in any form or by any means, electronic, mechanical, photocopying, recording, or otherwise, without the prior written permission of the publisher.

All ideas, recommendations, methods, techniques, principles, training, or subjects mentioned are for informational and educational purposes only. Because of the intangible and external influences that may bear on the use of these ideas and suggestions in any application, and the absolute necessity for a totally integrated planning effort, the authors and the publisher make no promises and accept no responsibility for the manner in which any of the information provided or contained herein may be applied, nor for any adverse effects that may result therefrom.

Recognizing the importance of preserving what has been written, it is the policy of Butterworth-Heinemann to have the books it publishes printed on acid-free paper, and we exert our best efforts to that end.

Library of Congress Cataloging-in-Publication Data

Gigliotti, Richard J.
    Emergency planning for maximum protection / Richard Gigliotti, Ronald Jason.
        p. cm.
    Includes bibliographical references and index.
    ISBN 0–409–90076–1
    1. Crisis management. 2. Employers' liability. I. Jason, Ronald
C. II. Title.
HD49.G54 1991
658.4—dc20   90–2347
                                                                   CIP

British Library Cataloguing in Publication Data

Gigliotti, Richard
    Emergency planning for maximum protection.
    1. Emergency services. Planning
    I. Title II. Jason, Ronald
    363

    ISBN 0–409–90076–1

Butterworth–Heinemann
80 Montvale Avenue
Stoneham, MA 02180

10 9 8 7 6 5 4 3 2 1

Printed in the United States of America

To Mr. and Mrs. Kissington,
our families,
our loved ones
and our very special friends.

Contents

Preface

Planning for emergencies has taken on a new importance in the 1990s. Concerns that did not exist before or were once not considered at all have now become topics of heated debate and subjects of concerted planning efforts. The realities of Chernobyl, Bhopal, Prince William Sound, and other such areas of catastrophe have combined to create greater awareness on the parts of those responsible for responding to such events. This, in turn, has resulted in progress to the point where we are just beginning to think about proactive responses that are planned, documented, practiced, and implemented if and as necessary.

The December 1988 issue of *Security* magazine reported that most Fortune 500 companies have no management plan for dealing with catastrophes. If one stops to think about it, they have had no need for a plan to deal with catastrophes, at least up to the present. Many, if not most, Fortune 500 companies made their mark before the advent of the contemporary phenomenon of litigation run amok. When these companies were emerging as forerunners, vicarious liability was merely a concept debated in quiet discussions on law school campuses. For the most part, the Fortune 500 symbolizes entrepreneurial acumen—individual contribution combined with team effort, a genuine concern for the organization, a management system based on rewards for contributions that secured the company's place in the economic order of things. The idea that individual responsibilities for such basic things as personal safety, for example, would be superseded by a system that holds the organization responsible for individual shortcomings was so totally foreign that, if it had existed at the time of their development, most of our top companies would never have exercised the initiative and enterprise necessary to accomplish great things.

Unfortunately, we now live in a world where it is foolish indeed for an organization, be it a Fortune 500 company, a small mom-and-pop operation, or a municipality to neglect its responsibilities to its members or to those over which it exercises control. Aside from the economic consequences, the moral considerations should more than justify anticipating and planning for events that could jeopardize people or their livelihoods. This book is intended to assist those persons charged with planning a response to any or all the risks to which a contemporary organization is exposed. It is hoped that the appendixes will be especially useful toward this end.

ACKNOWLEDGMENTS

We would like to express our sincere appreciation to Debie DeDomenico and Lynette Joseph for their outstanding typing support and to Dennaye Garbati and Lisa Jackson for their able assistance. Very special thanks to Diane Lubik, "Kristen Rostand," in recognition for her support and encouragement during a turbulent period. We would also like to recognize the following individuals for their encouragement, support, assistance, tolerance, and/or friendship during what at times proved to be a very difficult undertaking: Dolores Bianco; Father Greg Fluet; Bob Kenahan (Rhode Island State Police [Ret.]); John and Karen L'Heureux; Dave Mitchell; Chief George Sicaras (Hartford Police Department [Ret.]); Chris DePellegrini and Steve Messemer of Colt Firearms; Major Walt Scholtz, Lieutenant John Caputo, Detective Ed Hidek, and Detective Paul Mallon of the Connecticut State Police Department; Jim Coney of General Dynamics Electric Boat Division; Special Agent Bill Butchka (Federal Bureau of Investigation); Gene McDonald, Walt Thoma, and John Edwards of Globe Security Systems; Chuck Gaskin of the U.S. Nuclear Regulatory Commission; George Stefans of the U.S. Department of Energy; Bill D'Urso and Nick DeFelice of Interdome in Washington, D.C.; Dianne Williams and Tricia Sauter, Mohegan Community College, Norwich, Connecticut; and Bob Gregg, Norma Kornacki, Armelde Womble, Jim Tommaselli, and George Raposa of UNC Naval Products.

Last, but certainly not least, we would like to thank Greg Franklin (again) and Kevin Kopp of Butterworth–Heinemann for their patience, understanding, commitment, and friendship.

Richard J. Gigliotti
Ronald C. Jason

Introduction

To the average person, planning is a routine act that may consist of deciding, after a quick study of available information, which program to watch on TV. In most cases, such planning is conducted in a haphazard manner often without a lot of conscious thought given to the subject thus making it prone to frequent change. It almost seems in many cases that routine planning is based on random actions.

But routine planning is not totally random. It is always being carried out in our personal lives to some extent or other. Daily planning involves an orderly schedule that maximizes the use of valuable time. At home, a person must schedule time for grocery shopping, picking up the dry cleaning, maintaining some sort of social interaction with friends, and other such tasks.

Another example of routine planning could involve getting the family car into the shop for a badly needed repair (which should have been done months ago). If the repair requires several days, an alternate plan must be developed to compensate for the loss of the vehicle no matter how temporary. If a second car is available, its use must be scheduled between the alternating needs of two or more drivers. Or provisions must be made for renting or borrowing a car or using public transportation. Without a vehicle in this day and age, the peace, tranquility, and organizational fabric of the family unit may quickly be tested to their limits.

This is how average citizens carry out routine planning. Imagine if you will, how we go about planning for an *extraordinary event*; something as simple as a family vacation. Arrangements have to be made for the necessary time off from work. Coordination with a number of persons is necessary to ensure minimum adverse impact in the workplace.

Once a vacation spot has been selected, what additional planning will be necessary to ensure a safe arrival and a problem-free stay? Perhaps the single biggest item in this plan is obtaining the financial resources. Is the money in the savings account, or must a loan be arranged? If a loan is necessary, has enough time been allotted for its processing? Is the vacation to be taken overseas? If so, what about passports, shots, or an adequate supply of special medicines that may be required by a family member? What about travel arrangements? What about hotel reservations? Has the address of the American embassy or consulate at the destination been obtained? These and myriad other details must all be taken into consideration when planning even such a relatively simple thing as a family vacation.

Routine planning is essential to maintaining a relatively problem-free, normal lifestyle. In addition, to ensure that our ability to maintain this life-style suffers no major setbacks, we must all plan for or take precautions to minimize the adverse effects of life's extraordinary events.

If your home and the personal possessions therein were to burn to the ground, the loss would be terrible. However, to prevent it from becoming an event of catastrophic proportions, adequate fire insurance is (or should be) maintained. By the same token, a prudent family maintains adequate life insurance. Special insurance policies may have been obtained that cover damage to the home or loss of personal property in the event of occurrences labeled "acts of God." This type of insurance is obviously desirable in those sections of the world where devastating natural events occur frequently. Again these are but a few examples of items that should be considered in one's personal life when planning for extraordinary events.

In our professional lives, to be truly successful, we must also plan not only for the routine occurrences but also for all extraordinary events. This requires a formal, systematic approach to ensure that a potential problem is examined from all possible angles. This planning ensures that we can respond to or compensate for any variation or degree of escalation. In many cases of routine planning, the problem to be surmounted is usually restricted to one department; however, it could overlap into other departments or, in some cases, effect the entire organization. But rather than in a disorganizing manner, such effect would be in a *day-to-day operation* manner.

When planning for extraordinary events, the expertise of other individuals, from both within and outside the organization, may be required to develop an adequate plan (depending on the problem to be solved and the results desired). When such coordination between personnel or corporate departments is necessary in the preparation of a plan, one individual must be given sole responsibility for plan preparation and implementation. This responsibility *must* be accompanied by:

- The necessary authority to obtain whatever personnel and material resources may be required
- The authority to implement the plan
- The authority to cut across the chain of command, if necessary

To be truly effective, such authority must derive from the senior company official. It must be clearly and formally communicated to all other level officials.

Depending on the severity of the threat and the thoroughness with which the plan has been prepared, it is conceivable to find an individual in middle management directing or delegating responsibilities to individuals who would normally be senior to the middle manager. A company may recognize that in certain situations a specific person, by virtue of background and training, may be the best person for the task at hand regardless of hierarchal position. To complete the plan, all other personnel supporting this person must likewise recognize that a team effort is necessary.

As we have hopefully illustrated, there is planning, and there is *PLAN-NING*. Anyone who fails to make the distinction is doing both himself and his organization a disservice. In the previous paragraphs, certain comparisons have been made between an individual's personal and professional planning. The reader should not assume this book has been structured only toward someone employed in the private sector. The authors intend that the principles outlined together with examples can be equally applied to any form of organization, whether it be private or public, small or large.

This book is divided into two main sections. The concepts of emergency planning in the first section are translated into actions that collectively form the response by an organization to an extraordinary event. The second section, the appendixes, form an essential part of this work. They capture the essence of emergency planning in a meaningful way and provide the reader with bases for individual emergency plans.

Emergency Planning
for Maximum
Protection

1

Defining the Terms

Before emergency planning in an organization can begin, basic or routine planning must be addressed. Whether routine planning is formally documented or whether it is handled on an *ad hoc* basis, it occurs in all organizations, and it can be best described as preparing for a regular course of action. We can extend the description by adding "normally anticipated." Thus the routine planning effort centers on preparing (and subsequently following) methods of handling routine and normally anticipated situations.

A municipality, for example, may have a basic plan for coping with a "normal" snowstorm that includes such considerations as the number of plows deployed, alternate side of the street parking regulations, and snow dumping sites. If, however, a "normal" snowstorm turns into a blizzard, the routine plan for coping may be insufficient or of negligible value.

This is not meant to underrate the value and importance of routine planning. Basic planning is a necessary and integral part of the organizational process. There are, however, considerations above and beyond such routine planning that must be considered and that extend to nonroutine situations that are variously referred to as emergencies, contingencies, crises, disasters, and catastrophes.

Emergencies may be defined as unexpected circumstances combined to create situations calling for immediate action. Though emergencies are more serious than routine situations, they are less serious than contingencies, crises, catastrophes, and disasters.

Examples of emergencies

Medical emergencies
- Major epidemics (influenza, rubella, typhus, cholera, and so forth)
- Mass food poisonings (intentional and unintentional)
- Blood shortages

Small, quickly controlled fires
- Private homes (single dwellings)
- Public buildings (damaging but not destructive to the point of services being affected)

1

- Business buildings (retail establishments and warehouses where potentiallly hazardous materials may be present)

Bomb threats

Accidents

- Industrial (including explosions)
- Nonindustrial (major traffic accidents involving multiple vehicles of multiple types and with or without serious injuries)
- Chemical/HAZMAT (acid leaks, noxious or toxic gas releases, and so forth)
- Power failures (very localized in nature and generally the result of a power distribution equipment breakdown, but could be the result of, or associated with, another type of emergency situation where a transformer is damaged or where service has been intentionally stopped to deal with another problem)

A *contingency* is an emergency that almost everyone knows is possible but not expected. Like emergencies, contingencies are more serious than emergencies and include:

- Winter storms (including ice, wind, and snow storms and blizzards)
- Floods (may be associated with a storm or could be the result of a dam break, ice jam on a river, snow melt, or so on)
- Hurricanes (actions restricted to preparation, damage control, and recovery)
- Power outages (events that affect large urban areas for long periods of time—generally for more than 90 minutes in daylight or 3 hours in darkness)
- Small uncontrolled fires (large commercial or public buildings, several adjacent single or multifamily dwellings, a business block)
- Forest fires
- Tornadoes (actions generally limited to warning and recovery)
- Earthquakes (actions generally limited to recovery)
- Civil disturbance (involves the breaking of laws; usually involves some form of violence including assaults, property damage, looting, and so forth)
- Public demonstration (generally law abiding in nature; may be some very low-level violence involving isolated individuals)
- Labor disputes/strikes (generally localized and peaceful in nature but always have the potential for developing quickly into a civil disturbance)

A *crisis* may be defined as an unsettled time or state of affairs whose outcome will make a difference.

Some examples of crises are:

- Large, quickly controlled fires (usually involving large areas but rapidly brought under control)

- Bombings/explosions (intentional or otherwise; the result of deliberate actions or circumstances unanticipated but with no criminal intent)
- Sabotage (always an intentional criminal act; its intensity and/or ramifications may vary, and it may take a variety of forms such as arson, vandalism, product tampering, and failing to meet mandated quality standards)
- Extortion (again always an intentional criminal act; motives may vary but the result is the same, that is, obtaining something by force or by undue or illegal power or a threat to commit same; product tampering may well be extortionate)
- Kidnapping (another intentional criminal act; usually motivated by a perpetrator's greed with the intended result being the payment of a ransom, or a demand for such a payment, for the safe return of the person abducted)
- Terrorist situations (covers a wide variety of situations that are generally localized in nature and have a less-than-national impact (albeit international ramifications); includes bombings, the taking of hostages, and other criminal acts)
- Product failures and liabilities (the failure of a product and/or the liability incurred by a company when any of its products or product designs is challenged because of injury or death resulting from use, abuse, or misuse of a particular product)
- Financial (financial crises may include hostile takeovers, situations resulting from criminal acts such as embezzlement by company officers, fraud, or mismanagement of organizations resulting in bankruptcy or Chapter 11 proceedings)
- Malpractice (the intentional failure to follow instructions and/or deliberate falsification of records. While of more concern to government installations and defense contractors, the results of malpractice can and do adversely affect any sort of organization and its business viability)

Another category of extraordinary events is *catastrophes*. We may define a catastrophe as a significant tragic event ranging from extreme mischance to total overthrow or ruin.

Yet another category of extraordinary events is *disasters*. These are the most serious types of extraordinary events because their effects are felt by a greater number of people than are those in the categories we have previously discussed. Disasters can be natural (or man-made) emergencies, contingencies, and crises that affect the surrounding community. They are usually localized events that spin out of control and end up posing a threat to uninvolved parties. A disaster would certainly include nuclear attack and radiation accidents and/or incidents. Perhaps the most dramatic recent example was the disaster at the Chernobyl nuclear reactor in the USSR on April 26, 1986. The causes and effects of this particular incident are still being evaluated and the effects will be felt for quite a long time.

As you can see, depending on the word used to describe an event, the magnitude of a nonroutine situation certainly can escalate in intensity if not in effect. There are differences in planning for regular courses of action and dealing with momentous tragic events. The first question to ask: "Is the organization prepared for anything out of the ordinary?"

For our purposes of planning (beyond routine), the differences in definitions are not so important as are the preparations. For all practical purposes, planning for extraordinary events includes certain generic elements or components since the basic difference between extraordinary events is intensity.

When it comes to emergency planning, it is most important that every conceivable action, reaction, response, resource, and emotion be considered even if such considerations may later be dismissed as nonessential to the emergency planning effort.

This methodology is the basic difference between routine and emergency planning—the consideration of every possible event and the formulation of preparations for each event beyond the norm. To plan for is to prepare for. One of the more difficult tasks for any organization is to anticipate and plan for all possible extraordinary events. This effort is as driven by the times as it is by societal aberrations. The Tylenol incident of a few years ago would probably have been unthinkable in 1950. Today just about anything is possible.

While anything is possible, a certain degree of probability must be attached to every extraordinary event that could affect an organization. Otherwise, much effort and many resources would be expended needlessly. There is dubious value, for example, in preparing an emergency plan for responding to a volcanic eruption in Connecticut.

Emergency planning can be quite boring; time consuming; and in some quarters, thought to be without merit (except for those events that are considered highly probable). Nonetheless, in today's society it is imperative. If an organization fails to evaluate its risks and vulnerabilities from extraordinary events, it does so at its own peril.

Paramount, when it comes to assessing risks and resulting emergency plans, is the inviolable precept that protecting people is the prime objective of the organization and its emergency planning effort. Protecting property and assets must always be secondary to protecting people. Far too many organizations reverse these priorities. The results have often been disastrous and have resulted in death; injury; property damage and, as is quite often the case, vicarious liability; civil penalties; and even criminal sanctions for the organization involved.

Protecting lives is most important when an event expands and may harm people outside its original sphere. There are certain actual (plant-affected) emergencies, contingencies, and crises, both natural and manmade, that could affect the surrounding community depending on the degree of severity. These include (again, depending on their severity): chemical/hazardous material (HAZMAT) incidents and accidents, transportation incidents and accidents, winter storms, floods, hurricanes, forest fires, tornadoes, earth-quakes, large uncontrolled fires, bombings/explosions, sabotage, terrorist acts, product failures and liability, and financial disasters. Most of these could be categorized as purely natural or manmade, there are also a number of events that fit neither category exclusively and that also require proper response plans. These are events that may be initiated by an action in one category but result in primary impact in the other category. An example of such an event is described in the next chapter.

2

An Example of an Extraordinary Event

This chapter will examine an extraordinary event at a job site initiated by an action in one category but resulting in primary impact in another category. The event is an ice storm or very heavy sleet that occurs about 4 P.M. on a weekday. The first obvious impact will be on departing employees who will be leaving the job site at approximately 4:30 P.M. Since the storm has begun so abruptly (for the purposes of this example), it is extremely unlikely that highway crews have even begun the necessary sanding and/or road salting operations. *Problem number one* is employee safety both on and off company property.

Because of the quick and violent manner in which this storm has developed, electrical utility lines are snapping and falling under the weight of accumulated ice and sleet or as trees and tree limbs become so heavy that they break.

Problem number two is a loss of commercial power. The manufacturing processes conducted at this site, or the municipal services provided here, are dependent upon a steady electrical supply. Loss of electrical power may cause adverse chemical reactions and the spoilage of certain products in various stages of processing (whether manufactured or perishable) and may severely curtail the provision of public services.

Problem number three associated with the situation deals with keeping essential processes in operation or keeping necessary public services in operation.

In making a decision at any level, a *branching* effect can be seen. That is, if employees do not drive personal vehicles to the affected site but rely rather on public transit, little or no time may be devoted to ensuring the safe exit of privately owned vehicles from the site. This would, in essence, eliminate the need for any further planning. However, if in fact all or most employees travel via automobiles from and to the work site, considerations could include:

7

- Recommendation to all employees that they remain at the work site until highway crews have completed sanding/salting operations
- Frequently updating prevailing weather conditions for those employees who choose to stay
- Having plant maintenance or municipal highway maintenance personnel sand/salt all sidewalks, parking lots, and access roads up to the point where site exits join public roadways.

At any of these points, a *branching* would occur since some decision must be made about procedures. For example, if all the employees chose to stay at the work site until safe road passage was assured, an assembly area would have to be designated if a second operating shift had taken the place of persons who would normally be departing. If a second shift was not being utilized, perhaps personnel could return to their work areas particularly if the work area were in an office setting. Another *branching* decision might involve the fact that the ice and sleet had prevented those personnel who made up the next operating shift from reaching the work site. Should the persons who had completed their work be asked to continue working until they were relieved by incoming personnel? Should the next operating shift be cancelled? How would personnel be notified that their shift had been cancelled and when to report to work thereafter?

The second problem noted in this example, that of the loss of commercial power, would reach a *branch* point if the site were equipped with a suitable emergency power system. If the site could generate its own power to continue necessary operations, no decision would need to be made regarding cancellation of shifts and the notification of employees. The issues of preventing loss of product or damage to equipment or providing essential municipal services would become irrelevant. A separate number of new decisions would, however, become necessary. Is there a qualified member of the Maintenance Department on site to ensure that the emergency generator will operate properly at all times? Is the fuel supply adequate for the anticipated period of commercial power interruption? Have arrangements been made for delivery of additional fuel *before* the current supply reaches a dangerously low level? Have appropriate management personnel been contacted and advised of the situation?

Problem number three requires its own separate actions that will also *branch*. If there are essential processes or services that require continuation, personnel and adequate power will be required. Arrangements must be made to hold personnel over, call them in early, ensure emergency power supplies (including the considerations noted above), and perhaps even notify government regulatory agencies. If there are no essential processes or services requiring continuation, nothing further need be done.

As can be seen, a *simple* event, such as an ice storm or heavy sleet—weather conditions that occur quite often in many parts of the country—can severely impact an organization.

In certain other areas of the country, ice storms or heavy sleet are rare occurrences and planning for such events may not be necessary. As we have mentioned elsewhere, any planning effort requires that the situations for which planning is being considered be evaluated for their degree of *probability* versus *possibility*. Prioritization or categorizing each event will make planning proceed much more smoothly. It would probably be a waste of effort to formulate a plan for dealing with an ice storm at a site in the southern part of Florida and may make as much sense as preparing plans for dealing with a tsunami in Cincinnati or a blizzard in Baton Rouge.

Naturally, plans should be structured to provide a graduated response to each situation as it may escalate in intensity or severity. The adage, "You don't use a sledge hammer to kill a mosquito" comes to mind as being very descriptive of plans that prescribe only a single course of action to meet each emergency. It is far better to establish operating parameters that clearly delineate the expected or accepted norms of performance. These parameters, when simply written and thoroughly understood by all personnel, will serve as boundaries and provide a means for quickly determining when a situation has become something out of the ordinary, and they will serve as a trigger to initiating emergency response plans if necessary or simply to alerting senior officials and/or initiating closer monitoring of the situation.

The following scenario provides a brief example of a graduated response that deals with a variation of the ice storm/heavy sleeting conditions previously proposed. Weather conditions quickly deteriorate and a fairly routine winter rain storm turns into freezing rain. The freezing rain develops approximately two hours before the end of the normal work day (or shift change period). Weather forecasters, however, do not believe that the icy coating on highways will be a major problem since it is being caused by a swiftly moving front followed by slightly warmer air. Telephone calls to the local storm control center indicate that road sanding and salting operations are underway and that no major difficulties are anticipated with traffic movement by the beginning of the rush hour.

At this point, a graduated response would be to simply continue to monitor the situation but to also begin sanding and salting all company parking lots, roadways and walkways. It would be prudent to convene a quick meeting among appropriate members of management to review emergency plans in the event the situation does not improve but in fact deteriorates. Individual areas that may need attention should be independently addressed to ensure a proper company response should one become necessary. Please note that the response measures implemented thus far are reasonable and cannot be considered excessive in light of the available information. Avoidance of the *sledge hammer* response to this situation, which in all probability would result in an immediate closing of the facility and the resultant placement of all employees out on the highways at a time when traveling is most dangerous, has allowed production to continue, provided a safe place for workers to wait for an improvement in road conditions, generally resulted in a positive feeling for the company by all employees, and avoided a great deal of wasted effort on the part of many managers and supervisors.

If the situation were to escalate in severity, proper response measures would be implemented thanks to management's foresight in ensuring that plans were reviewed, that key personnel were available, and that necessary equipment and other resources were ready.

Plans for dealing with any situation, whether natural or manmade, must therefore provide for an escalated response in proportion to the increased severity of the situation.

It is therefore prudent for the emergency planner to consider virtually all possible contingencies with an eye to the results if any particular event is not addressed and/or responded to in a timely, appropriate, and effective manner to preclude events of lesser magnitude from becoming events of greater magnitude.

3

What Is Crisis Management?

"What is Crisis Management?" This is a good question—what does it mean to you? Does it mean that we wait for a crisis to occur then do whatever must be done to correct the situation? Unfortunately, this is all too often the case *within* some companies or within the departments of some municipal agencies.

It is quite possible that the corporate office, the site manager, or municipal leaders have developed in-house (or have had developed by an outside consultant) a comprehensive plan for dealing with most anticipated crises. In many cases, however, the plan is simply circulated to all department heads or senior staff managers who, even though they may not be directly involved in a crisis management role, are made aware of its provisions "so no one's feelings get hurt." After the individuals to whom the plan has been circulated have done their duty by "read(ing) and initial(ing)" the plan, it is relegated to a file cabinet drawer somewhere where it remains hidden from view, waiting for the call to action that may not come for many years.

In the interim, individuals who were appointed as members of the original site Crisis Management Team (CMT) have been following their own career patterns and may no longer be a part of the crisis management structure. Their replacements have hopefully been required to make themselves familiar with the plan(s) developed for dealing with crises. In many cases, however, this is not done usually through simple oversight or because the concept of crisis management has assumed a status comparable to that of the lost continent of Atlantis—everyone has heard that it exists, but no one knows what became of it. The old bromide, "Use it or lose it!", has some applicability in this case.

If the intent is to have a *meaningful* crisis management program, it must be paid *much more* than mere lip service. Someone, somewhere, sometime has gone to a great deal of trouble to develop the necessary plans to deal with the crises that could be *reasonably* expected to befall the individual organization. Let us not let their efforts go to waste. Once the plan has been developed, its individual responsibilities must be assigned. In most cases, assignment of individual responsibilities is very clear. For example, the Number One and

Number Two individuals in the organization should automatically be assigned to the CMT. Others who should also be designated as team members include senior staff individuals responsible for controlling financial assets, maintenance or facility engineering, operations, security, and personnel. If these responsibilities have not been assigned in the plan(s), it is something senior management must do *by individual name or title* as one of its first priorities. A flaw of this magnitude could make a plan totally worthless.

After the CMT has been selected, it must be assembled and given a detailed briefing about what is expected from each individual or department if a crisis occurs. Questions should be encouraged to avoid problems before they occur. At this initial team get-together for briefing, each member should be given a copy of the plan that deals with his or her particular area(s) of responsibility. Another meeting should be scheduled for far enough in the future to ensure that all members of the Crisis Management Team have had enough time to make themselves very familiar with their portion(s) of the plan(s). In most cases, the responsibilities will be the same regardless of the nature of the crisis thus ensuring simplified procedures and a good understanding of responsibilities.

At the next meeting, all questions or problems should be frankly discussed and clearly resolved. All resolution(s) should be written out and either appended to the plan(s) or the plan(s) should be changed to reflect the deviations from the initial concept(s). So far so good, but knowing what needs to be done in a crisis situation is far different from actually doing it. To ensure a truly professional response to a crisis situation, the CMT must be periodically "exercised." It is suggested that the most senior members of the CMT develop scenarios involving situations that could realistically occur with which the CMT would be expected to deal. This is a topic that will be discussed in greater detail later.

The object of these crisis scenarios is clearly not to embarrass anyone but rather to find out where problems could occur if the situation were real. Once the potential problems have been identified, steps can be taken to ensure they do not occur or, if they should occur, can be effectively dealt with. These training scenarios could even be videotaped and used in an after-action critique.

Periodic exercise of the CMT will ensure that a necessary *edge* is maintained. It will also ensure that the individual membership of the CMT is kept current and that routine personnel changes will not result in a CMT whose members are unaware of their responsibilities in the event of a crisis.

The CMT must be ready, at relatively short notice, to assemble in a pre-designated location equipped with whatever supplies, equipment, and communications are necessary for the CMT's use. Once it has been activated, the CMT, under the general direction of the most senior member present, will take whatever action it considers necessary to safeguard personnel, to minimize damage or loss, and to return the facility, organization, or municipality to normal as quickly as possible. This may require granting authority to individual CMT team members, authority that may not be present in their routine assignments. To deal effectively with the crisis, CMT members *must* have the authority to cut through the red tape present in *every* organization. A great deal of this expediting will come about through coordination among the CMT team members. It is important that each person understand that no one member of the CMT is more important than any other—they are a "team," and, by definition, *they must work together!*

Now back to the original question, "What *is* Crisis Management?" It is the ability of an organization to deal quickly, efficiently, and effectively with contingency operations with the goal of reducing the threat to human health and safety, the loss of public or corporate property, and adverse impact on continued normal business or operations. To accomplish this goal, the organization must

1. Prepare formal plans that realistically address all potential crises that could befall the organization. These plans must be as complete and detailed as possible.
2. Implement a formal program to appoint a CMT consisting of members whose expertise in certain areas contributes significantly to overall minimizing of the situational effects or to recovery operations.
3. Assign individual responsibilities to the members of the CMT. When and where necessary, spell out the authority of each team member and establish a formal CMT organization chart.
4. Establish a formal method of emergency notification and recall of all CMT members.
5. Establish an emergency command center that contains all necessary communications capability, work areas, plans, blueprints, and so forth.
6. Test a portion of the plan periodically (at least semiannually), involving the CMT members.
7. Update and modify the plans as required following each exercise.
8. Assimilate new members of the CMT into the organization as quickly as possible to ensure the high quality service necessary from the team.

These are the basic elements of a successful Crisis Management Program.

4

Defining
an Organization's Needs

An integral part of any emergency plan preparation is a preliminary survey to determine exactly what vulnerabilities must be addressed in order to meet the plan goals. Before a decision is made to conduct a preliminary vulnerability survey, a need (or particular problem area), prompting such a survey must have already been identified.

The need(s) that prompt a vulnerability survey are varied and can range from the patently obvious to the very subtle. Planning for the obvious dangers include those of natural or manmade origin, examples of which are presented in Chapter 2. Those items, however, that at first glance do not appear to present any great danger to an organization may in fact contain the seeds of a potentially catastrophic event. If a problem area is not identified or is incorrectly diagnosed, it follows that it will either be dismissed out of hand or will receive minimal attention in the plan preparation process.

With no plans (or insufficient plans) for dealing with a particular problem, the potential for a rapid, and sometimes uncontrollable, escalation is present. Perhaps one of the most overworked, yet most often disregarded, early-warning signs is the phrase, "You know, this *could* be a problem." If someone makes this statement, then you *have* a problem until it has been painstakingly examined from all possible angles and either confirmed as a problem, or assigned a probability weight so low as to make it a matter of no further concern.

The first step in developing a plan to deal with extraordinary events is to make the most comprehensive list possible of *all* the types of events that could occur. Granted some of the items will appear unlikely in the extreme, but include them nonetheless. Then break the list into events that are the results of actions initiated by people, natural events, or "Acts of God." The next step is to rank each item on the list from 1 to 10 with 10 being those incidents that have the highest degree of probability of occurring and 1, the lowest.

Naturally the degrees of probability will differ according to location or other factors. For example, the probability that swarms of locusts will plague

New York City is low, and the lasting effect on the city (should it occur) would be slight. Therefore, New York City *could* develop a plan for dealing with such an event, but because of the unlikelihood of occurrence and the minimal damage potential, little if any time or effort should be devoted to development of this plan. In the grain-belt states, however, a locust invasion could have catastrophic results. In this case, a plan *must* be prepared.

Despite one's best efforts to assess all possible vulnerabilities and to develop a complete emergency plan that takes into account all contingencies, situations may still arise that are so far beyond the realm of probability that little, if any, contemplation has ever been given them.

Establishing the basic needs of any organization is fairly easy. They include: protecting the health and safety of personnel (both employees and the general public), safeguarding of company (or public) property and assets, minimal interruption in operations or services, and preservation of the public confidence in the product or services provided. Once the basic needs have been established, the first part of the vulnerability survey or evaluation can begin.

From *what* must the health and safety of personnel be protected? From *what* must property and assets be safeguarded? What *types* of interruptions in operations could occur? What causes could result in loss of public confidence with the product or services provided? Once these questions have been answered, the planning process can commence.

Probably the best approach would be to gather all department heads and other members of site management, to charge them with the responsibility for evaluating their individual operations, and to let their imaginations loose on developing a list of items they feel could adversely impact on their particular areas. It should be stressed that this is only a preliminary list and that *all* possibilities should be included, no matter how remote the probability. The more detail these personnel can include in their assessments, the better.

Once the individual assessments have been completed, another meeting should be conducted. It will be found that a great many concerns are common within the group. These will automatically become items for closer study and evaluation. Those items that are more obscure or that may impact only a certain part of the organization will be individually addressed. Because everyone is an individual, various reactions can be expected when individual concerns are subjected to group scrutiny. Some people may become defensive and feel that their personal veracity is being questioned or even attacked. Others may feel that their concern is inconsequential and not worthy of further discussion. *Most* individuals will address the issue in an objective manner, give it an honest evaluation, and know that if a concern is there its ramifications could very well extend into areas affecting other departments or operations. The issue deserves to be presented to the broadest spectrum of organization "thinkers and doers."

This review will result in some additional items being included with those previously (and automatically) accepted for further study and evaluation, as credible concerns. Others will be rejected for a variety of reasons. This should be a fairly short and straightforward process.

The group of concerns that make the first cut will now be subjected to more detailed examination. Few, if any, will be rejected at this stage. A determination must be made about each concern's degree of *possibility* and its occurrence versus its degree of *probability*. Once a prioritized list has been established, preparation of the emergency plans to deal with each contingency can commence. It makes little difference at this stage (except in the adverse impact possibilities) on whether the emergency situation for which plans are being prepared fits into the parameters established for an *emergency*, a *contingency*, a *crisis*, or a *disaster*.

In most cases, the very obvious dangers can be quickly and easily addressed. For example, a plan for dealing with a fire will be fairly well defined and is often simply a matter of updating an existing plan or adapting a plan in existence at another facility or within another organization. The secondary and subsequent parts of a fire protection plan, however, will be tailored to the individual organization since they must address site-specific concerns such as relocation of personnel and operations, repairs and restoration, emergency acquisition of equipment and material to return operations to normal as quickly as possible, temporary personnel reorganization and reallocation of personnel resources, or even a list of personnel to be furloughed until operations can be resumed. The number and composition of the addenda to a basic fire protection plan is up to the individual organization and is only governed in scope and detail by the amount of planning effort put into it and the results expected from it.

When they are preparing emergency plans, responsible personnel must avoid becoming *locked in* on the *usual* emergencies. In todays litigious society, many larger companies and municipalities have a plan for dealing with lawsuits filed against them. Such a plan should be seriously considered by *all* emergency planners, regardless of the size of the organization for which the plans are being formulated. In many cases, the plan may be nothing more than a policy statement that contains a standard public response suitable for publication while actual handling of a lawsuit is done by legal professionals and/or by an insurance carrier.

Another possibility for which many companies are preparing emergency plans deals with hostile takeover attempts. In preparing such plans, careful consultation with legal and financial experts is a must.

A third possibility for emergency planning with which many companies and municipalities now find themselves faced deals with terrorism. There are a number of excellent books on the subject that should be read by anyone who is contemplating or actively involved in planning for dealing with terrorist activities against public or private facilities. In addition, a large number of "terrorism experts" have recently come into existence who are ready to offer their services to assist in the preparation of such plans or the training of site personnel to deal with the threat. If hiring *any* consultant is contemplated, we recommend that the credentials and credibility of anyone under consideration be carefully checked.

Perhaps a crisis most captivating to the public imagination is that of a nuclear emergency. We are all familiar with the names Three Mile Island and Chernobyl. These two names represent the locations of the two worst nuclear accidents in the history of commercial nuclear power generation. While thousands of miles apart and separated by several years, the response to these accidents illustrates the necessity for having a thoroughly thought-out plan ready in the event of an incident involving the uncontained release of radiation. Steven Fink gives a brief but telling description of what happened at Three Mile Island. The Kemeny Commission Report took six months to conclude that "a series of events—compounded by equipment failures, inappropriate procedures, and human errors and ignorance—escalated (the accident) into the worst crisis yet experienced by the nation's nuclear power industry."[1]

While the Kemeny Commission report found that the proximate cause of this accident was the result of human error (compounded by other contributing factors), the result of the accident was that most of the radiation was contained onsite, that what radiation that did escape the site was low level and caused no long-term contamination of the surrounding area, and perhaps most importantly, that no one died or even suffered serious injury. Was this simply the result of luck or pure chance? Perhaps, but isn't the word *luck* often used to describe an occurrence that was really brought about by a lot of hard work and thorough planning?

Somewhere, at some time, the designers of this reactor realized that there *perhaps* existed the remote possibility that there *could* be an accident involving their equipment. Therefore they designed multiple backup systems to help prevent an accident, but they went even further in their planning. Anticipating that *all* of their systems could fail, they also designed a containment vessel in which the reactor sits, which will, in the event of a radiological accident, contain the resulting release of radiation within its steel and reinforced concrete walls. This is an excellent example of planning—do everything you can to keep the accident from occurring (or the crisis from developing), but also plan that, if all of your best efforts at prevention are unsuccessful, how the situation can best be mitigated.

Contrast the incident at Three Mile Island, however, with what occurred at the Chernobyl nuclear generating station in the Soviet Union approximately seven years later.

The accident at Chernobyl started at 1:23 A.M. on Saturday, April 26 (1986), when . . . the reactor's (power) suddenly increased during a

---

1. Stephen Fink, *Crisis Management—Planning for the Inevitable* (New York: American Management Association, 1986).

scheduled shutdown of the fourth unit. The considerable emission of steam and subsequent reaction resulted in the formation of hydrogen, its explosion, damage to the reactor and the associated radioactive release.[2]

This description, drawn from a specialist's report, was given by Mikhail Gorbachev, general secretary of the Communist party of the USSR, in his televised May 14 speech on the accident.

The hydrogen explosions caused extensive damage and fire on the ceiling of the *machine hall,* which is the portion of the reactor building directly above the core. This portion has an exceptionally high ceiling, to accommodate the fueling machine. One Soviet press report suggested that the fire might have spread up the walls of the building along a plastic surface coating that is used extensively in Soviet nuclear installations. An article in Pravda, based on interviews with the firefighters, graphically described the roof blazing 30 meters above the reactor and the firefighters battling ankle-deep in molten bitumen.[3]

Another article states that

The Chernobyl calamity occurred, ironically, in the course of a safety test. According to the report, workers were trying to determine how long the reactor's turbine generators would continue to operate as a result of inertia in the event of an unforeseen reactor shutdown. To prevent the automatic safety systems from interfering with the experiment, the technicians disconnected them, opening the way for a chain of fatal mishaps.[4]

At 1:23 A.M. April 26, the workers began the actual experiment by stopping power to the turbine. Just prior to that, the flow of the water that normally cooled the reactor was reduced and certain safety devices were disengaged. The reactor immediately began to overheat dangerously, but since the emergency cooling system had been shut off some 12 hours earlier, there was no backup. Within seconds, there was a tremendous power surge that caused two explosions, blew the roof off the reactor building and ignited more than 30 fires around the plant. The damaged reactor core and the graphite surrounding it began burning at temperatures as high as 2800°F. The fire sent a plume of radioactive debris into the upper atmosphere while Soviet firefighters in helicopters frantically tried to extinguish the blaze by dumping 5000 tons of boron, lead and other material on the reactor core. They did not succeed in putting out the fire until 12 days after the accident.[5]

---

2. "The Chernobyl Accident," *Nuclear News* 29, no. 8 (1986): 87.

3. Ibid.

4. Michael B. Serrill *et al.* "Anatomy of a Catastrophe," *Time,* 1 September 1986, p. 26. Copyright 1986 Time Inc. Reprinted by permission.

Ibid., p. 27.

In the subsequent official investigation, it became apparent that adequate safeguards had been designed into the reactor construction to prevent an ordinary accident. This was *not*, however, an ordinary occurrence. By their intentional failure to obey the established operating procedures and by their actions in disabling automatic control and safety systems, the reactor operators set up a situation that went far beyond the design basis threat envisioned by the plants designers thereby making the accident inevitable.

The effects of this disaster went beyond the physical confines of reactor number four at the Chernobyl power generating station, reaching far into the Soviet countryside and across boundaries into other European nations. The long-term results of contamination of air, land, water, wildlife, and livestock are yet to be fully realized or even determined. And what of the long-term effects on the thousands of persons who lived within the zone of highest radioactive contamination? Beyond the fact that they were uprooted from their homes with only a few hours notice and had to leave nearly all of their personal possessions behind, they have been moved and relocated to areas of the country that may be totally foreign to them. In many of these cases, a return to their homes within the danger zone may never happen because of the difficulty of clearing up the contamination. In other areas, return may happen someday, but that someday may be a long time coming.

The bottom line results of both the U.S. and Soviet investigations into the respective causes of these nuclear accidents put the blame squarely on the shoulders of the operators who were in charge of plant operations at the time of the incidents, in other words, on human error. Unfortunately, all the planning in the world, no matter how detailed, cannot completely compensate for human inattention or intentional circumvention of safety systems. The differences in design between the reactors at Three Mile Island and at Chernobyl have been discussed, and it is believed that the difference in design had a great deal to do with the differences in the extent of radioactive release. Judging by the information available, it appears that the Soviet authorities were, in all probability, caught *flat-footed* by the extent of the reactor damage and massive release of radioactive material. It is fairly certain that they also had emergency plans in place. It is apparent, however, that these plans were not designed to deal with a problem of the actual magnitude experienced.

The point to be made is that no plan (or mechanical design) is totally foolproof. As long as fools are in this world who choose not to obey the rules or who intentionally circumvent automatic controls or safety equipment that has been put into place to save the fool's life, there is nothing any of us can do except curse the fools for their stupidity as we go about cleaning up their messes and making things right again.

5

Assessing an Organization's Vulnerabilities

Vulnerability phases, both the initial phase prior to plan preparation and the second, more detailed, phase after plan preparation to ensure that nothing has been overlooked and that all vulnerabilities are adequately addressed in the plan, must extend beyond the boundaries of the entity for which the emergency plan has been generated. For example, if plans are being prepared for an industrial facility, consideration must be given to the area surrounding the plant site. If this industrial facility were located in the midst of a number of other manufacturing facilities, could a fire spread to this facility from a neighboring company? If so, how can the facility best be protected, and how can damage be minimized? If the industrial facility was located in a single large building with a number of other businesses, could a labor dispute at another company result in blocking the access of uninvolved personnel? Prior planning for such an emergency could involve establishing liaison with police, identifying alternate building access routes, and, perhaps, even employees parking away from the site with arrangements made to bus them in.

In certain parts of the United States, seasonal weather conditions may very well require a company or a municipality to periodically deal with blizzards, floods, earthquakes, hurricanes, tornados, and other natural phenomena. For a manufacturing facility, these plans may require the early release of employees from work, call-in of employees during off-shift periods, cancellation of shifts, and, depending on the adverse impact on the company of the weather conditions, even a layoff of personnel should damage prevent a quick return to normal operation. In addition, orders and deliveries for materials might have to be canceled and scheduled deliveries of company product either rescheduled or canceled. If only a part of the facility were to receive damage, arrangements to move affected parts of the operation to an alternate facility might be necessary as would the emergency replacement of machinery and/or equipment, while the remainder of the company continued in production even if on a somewhat limited basis.

21

Such plans should be *layered*, or otherwise provide for an escalation of response. The following is an example of a single situation as it escalates through four conditions from emergency through disaster.

1. A power failure is experienced and all essential public services or the industrial facilities, manufacturing/production facilities, are affected. This would be an *emergency*.

2. The power failure has required the substitution of manpower for machines in controlling traffic or the use of alternate sources of power—for example, the activation of emergency generators in hospitals and other facilities requiring an uninterruptable power supply. Normal operations continue, albeit at a much reduced pace or in a modified manner. This would be a *contingency*.

3. The power failure is more than 16 hours in duration. Industrial facilities have had to cancel shifts; public transit, which is dependant on electric power, may not be operating; fire alarm pull boxes are not operating; many people may have been stranded in elevators and require rescuing or are otherwise unable to find a way out of unfamiliar surroundings easily. This would be a *crisis*.

4. The power failure is now into its second day/night; people (particularly the elderly) are stranded in their homes without heat/air conditioning. Emergency services agencies are being inundated with calls for assistance and for transportation of emergency cases to medical facilities; they may, in fact, be overtaxed. Fires have broken out at many widely separated points, and they cannot be reported and reponded to expeditiously. Police and other emergency services personnel have been on continuous duty for nearly the entire length of the power failure, and personnel are being relieved to obtain some needed rest. Other than this, there are no backup or reserve forces available. Widespread public disorder and/or looting has been reported. A larger part of the private sector could very well become affected at this stage by one of any number of adverse events that were initiated at the industrial facility previously mentioned, and because of a delay in reporting and/or emergency agencies' inability to respond, the facility's viability is lost, effectively putting a number of people out of work and possibly causing the company to relocate or go out of business. This is a *disaster*.

In preparing plans for any organization, an honest appraisal must be made of its vulnerabilities. This will provide a base from which all planning may proceed. While there are undoubtedly individuals within the organization who are well qualified to conduct such a vulnerability survey, there is a tendency among many senior managers to dismiss the sometimes dire warnings of in-house personnel as being unnecessarily alarmist, despite the fact that it is these same individuals who are most familiar with the problems likely to be encountered and who have primary responsibility for dealing with them. This is perhaps, the greatest source of dissatisfaction among professionals who are charged with the day-to-day operations of an organization. These individuals, perhaps more than any others within the organization, are *most* aware of the problems but find that their opinions are disregarded and their recommendations, dismissed. The old bromide "prophets in their own land" comes to mind in these cases and seems to sum up this often encountered situation well. This propensity by some senior managers is often symptomatic of their self-imposed disassociation with the reality of day-to-day operations. When this is the likely situation in attempting to make senior management totally aware of the areas in which problems may very well be encountered, it may be desirable to obtain the services of an independent evaluator. (It is often puzzling and more than a little demoralizing to those officials or professionals who must deal with these problems to find that their opinions and recommendations are ignored while those *same* opinions and recommendations put forth by an individual from outside the organization who in all probability is being paid handsomely for the services, are taken as pronouncements from the mount.) In selecting such an individual, any number of consultants are willing to provide their services in this area, and in many cases, the services provided are worth the price. There are also a number of self-described experts, however, who can be most charitably described as charlatans. It therefore behooves any organization contemplating the services of an independent vulnerability evaluator to *evaluate* the evaluator. Ideally, the person selected should be thoroughly familiar, either through current employment or by past association, with a similarly sized organization in the same or in a closely allied field. If the organization for which the survey is to be performed is a municipality, then service with civil government of similar size and demographics would be desirable. Naturally, selection of an individual with a *proven* track record in conducting vulnerability surveys would be the goal. The individual selected (or the individuals if the magnitude of the survey is beyond that which could reasonably be expected of a single person) should be given access to whatever information, areas, and personnel necessary short of that information and those areas that may divulge company proprietary or government classified information or that could, if it became general knowledge, aid an adversarial group in any unauthorized actions against the organization. It is further recommended that any contract or agreement with such an *outside* evaluator, should contain a detailed but clearly worded nondisclosure clause.

Suitable working space and logistical support should be provided as should access to various professional personnel within the organization who may be consulted on certain technical/logistical aspects of perceived vulnerabilities or contemplated remedies. A schedule of periodic progress reports/ briefings should be established and documented. If the organization is serious about addressing its vulnerabilities, senior management officials will be there. This may very well be the yardstick by which the commitment of senior management may be measured. If there is no interest exhibited in learning where the weaknesses lie, there will not in all probability be a great deal of interest in, or enthusiasm for support of, the recommended solutions.

The preliminary survey will generally consist of a detailed inspection of the facility or other area for which recommendations are sought. Such inspection should not necessarily be restricted to those areas that are easily accessible but should include normally inaccessible areas such as a plant roof, basement, warehouse, and records storage areas. If the survey is being conducted for a municipality, the evaluator(s) may wish to visit sewage pumping stations, for example, to determine the equipment capabilities for handling a sudden infusion of storm drain water, or the capacity to handle normal demands should there be a protracted period of equipment outage. Where housing and/or manufacturing facilities are located close to railroad lines used to move toxic or hazardous chemicals, records of prevailing winds may be requested as well as evacuation route maps. Once evacuation routes have been determined, actual travel over these routes is recommended to ascertain if they are indeed able to handle the demands that will be placed on them in the event of an actual emergency. When homes, schools, business centers, or manufacturing facilities are located on takeoffs or approaches to airports, a study should be conducted to determine what the response time will be for essential emergency services personnel and equipment should an aircraft crash in one of these areas. Will there be an adequate number of responding fire trucks? Will these fire trucks be equipped to deal with a fire that may very well be fueled by not only the aircraft's fuel tanks but also by ruptured natural gas lines? Have fire personnel been trained in situations of this type? Is there a method for quickly obtaining public utility emergency crews to shut down ruptured gas lines and severed electrical utility lines? How quickly, and in what numbers, can ambulances be directed to the scene? Can area hospitals handle an incident involving a great number of casualties? Has a site to which personnel who must be evacuated from the area of such an accident been identified? Can quick access to this emergency evacuation site be gained? These are but a *very few* of the questions that should be addressed in a situation of this type. Each particular vulnerability identified will generate many of its own questions or considerations that must be answered. In many situations, a plan developed for one type of emergency is just as usable in another. For example, the evacuation of a building (or a section of a town or city) because of a fire would be just as applicable to an evacuation made necessary by release of a toxic chemical. Imposition of water rationing because of a drought would follow the same guidelines as if the available water supply were to become contaminated and require switching to a backup supply of limited capacity. The early release of private or public employees in the event of a massive power failure could be regulated by the same plan used in the event of a snow storm.

Once the vulnerabilities have been identified, the next step is to categorize them as either "probable" or "possible." Once divided into these two categories, the vulnerabilities should be rank-ordered within each column, from highest to lowest degree of probability or possibility. During the recommended periodic briefings to senior management, these lists should be presented and the pros and cons of each identified item debated. It will be the responsibility of senior managers, to determine which of the identified vulnerabilities warrant development of contingency plans. This may involve moving some items among columns, but after their decision is rendered, a memorandum of understanding should be prepared and distributed to all parties concerned. The next stage will be the actual preparation of contingency plans to deal with those items that have been identified as most urgent by senior management. At this point, no further briefings are considered necessary until the final plan is ready for presentation.

6

A General or Event-Specific Plan: Assumptions and Decisions

In developing any emergency plan, a decision must be made early in the planning stages about whether the plan will be general in nature or event specific.

Depending upon the emergency the plan is being developed to meet, the desired plan, and indeed the plan that will best suit the needs of most users, is one that in a practical sense lies between *general* and *event specific*. If, for example, a company or governmental entity, is developing a plan for dealing with a flood, a general plan will, by its very nature, fail to address a number of small but important points. A general plan will probably provide for some sort of notification system to advise personnel who may be affected by the emergency situation of the danger and of what they should do. A general plan will designate an emergency command center, emergency shelters, provide for necessary food and health and welfare items, and may even address post-situation recovery.

An event-specific plan, on the other hand, picks up where a general plan ends and provides, often in great detail, information on every possible contingency that may be associated with the emergency. This type of plan is often formal and very structured. It sets forth individual responsibilities, establishes timetables, and spells out, "Who does what, when."

There are definite advantages as well as disadvantages to each type of plan. A general plan, is adaptable to a wide variety of emergencies although it will be somewhat lacking in finite details, leaving these up to the judgment of the individuals whose task will be to make the plan work. An event-specific plan, while not generally adaptable to a wide variety of emergencies, will be the product of a great deal of preevent planning, which has taken into consideration all probable (and perhaps some improbable) contingencies and has detailed procedures for dealing with each of these probabilities.

If the organization whose task it is to implement the emergency plan is small and the number of personnel with whom it must deal is similarly limited, then a general plan is perhaps the best choice. The relatively uncomplex general plan can be easily modified to fit the organization's needs and/or meet new and probably unforeseen conditions that can, and usually do, arise in any emergency. The flexibility of individual emergency managers is not limited by the definitive environment present when they are following an event-specific plan. Thus they are free to explore and/or take advantage of opportunities that may suddenly present themselves.

An event-specific plan generally works well in very large organizations (corporate giants as well as public agencies) where the personnel staffing and available resources can adequately support a complex operation. In cases of this sort, the event-specific emergency plan will have been laboriously prepared and will assign responsibilities to departments (or the governmental equivalent), provide for necessary equipment and supplies, establish a chain of command, and spell out, often in a matrix format, what is to be done, who is to do it, when it must be done, who must assist in getting it done, and, what follow-up action is required after it is done. For large organizations with the personnel and physical material resources, an event-specific plan is often ideal since it establishes a presence, which acts as a subliminal message to those persons who are turning to it for aid, that they will be cared for and protected and that there is still order in a world suddenly turned to chaos.

The choice between preparation of a general or event-specific plan, is therefore a matter of personal choice but should be arrived at only after a decision has been made as to which will best suit the needs of the organization based upon the numbers of persons to be served, the number of personnel available to staff the emergency organization, and the availability of resources to adequately support the emergency effort.

7

Some Essential Elements

Once the needs and vulnerabilities of the site to be protected (be it a single private building, industrial or retailing complex, or municipal building) have been determined, the natural progression is to prepare a plan for dealing with the probabilities. In any plan, certain essential elements must be included. If the plan is being prepared for a private concern, company policy as it may apply to the situation should preface any directed actions. If the plan deals with an emergency likely to be faced by a municipal government, a statement of purpose may be inserted. In either case, the authority that requires preparation of the plan should be cited. Once this "boiler plate" is out of the way, actual plan composition can begin. It is recommended that the known vulnerabilities that the plan is being designed to address be identified. It is further recommended that legal counsel review this section (and indeed *all* plan sections) to determine defensibility should at some future point a lawsuit be initiated due to the action or inactions of responsible parties under the plan.

Since the initiation of emergency response plans or contingency plans is not an action that would, under ordinary conditions, be arbitrarily taken by a single individual, it is probable that a Crisis Management Team (CMT) will be formed. Members of the CMT will be drawn from senior and upper-level management in the private section and from department/agency heads in the public sector. The composition of the CMT should be restricted to a manageable level and should include those who can provide meaningful support in meeting the emergency. Leadership of the CMT is seldom a question since the senior official present will automatically assume this function. A wise leader, however, will recognize that many different types of emergencies may better be handled by a subordinate with the role of the CMT intentionally limited to one of technical and/or logistical support and planning for recovery operations. A major fire, for example, could probably best be handled by the head of the maintenance department (or whatever other internal division is charged with plant fire protection) rather than having the company president or plant management assume control at the scene since he or she, may not be completely qualified to act in that capacity (or interested in doing so). The mayor of a city will not assume personal control of firefighting operations at the scene of a fire at a high-rise building but will leave this work to the "professionals." This does not mean that the on-scene commander has total autonomy. This individual *must* maintain communications with the CMT and provide periodic situation reports. The CMT, for its part, must avoid overloading the on-scene commander with requests for information to the point where the commander is effectively removed from control and becomes nothing more than a spectator/reporter.

On the subject of communications, it is essential that dependable methods of communicating between the on-scene commander, the CMT, and any other department or agency directly involved in an auxiliary or direct-support role be maintained at all times during the course of the emergency situation. This will probably require the establishment of a radio network especially where the situation may require the movement of personnel. When the establishment of a radio network system is contemplated, consideration should be given to the acquisition of quality equipment with dependability, not price, as the prime concern. Base units as well as portable units should be required, taking into consideration that some units may be out of service at any given time. Due consideration of such a situation will ensure the acquisition of extra units to meet any anticipated demand. If it is anticipated that most emergency situations may be rather fluid in that a great deal of movement over great distances may be necessary, the most powerful hand-held units available should be purchased. Serious consideration should also be given to multichannel units that allow cross-communication as necessary between various agencies that may also be working on the same problem. Base stations should be of sufficient wattage to ensure reliable communications with antennas sited at the most advantageous points. If it is anticipated that mobile or hand-held radio transmitters/receivers may be used at great distances from the controlling base units, the use of radio repeaters may become necessary. Base units and repeater sites (if utilized) may require an uninterruptible power supply to carry the necessary load should purchased power fail. This uninterruptible power supply might consist of storage batteries and/or on-site electrical generators. *All* batteries, for the hand-held units as well as those that may be part of the uninterruptible power supply, should be periodically maintained to ensure necessary dependability when they are needed in an emergency situation. If an onsite electrical generator is installed, it too should receive periodic attention. A preventive maintenance program is recommended as is periodic operation under load. Normally this is something that can be done once a year, but more frequent operational tests are highly desirable. The fuel supply for the emergency generator should be of sufficient capacity/quantity to support around-the-clock operation for at least 48 hours. Any emergency plan should also contain a provision to ensure that the fuel supply for the generator is replenished well in advance of its being exhausted and, if necessary, periodically resupplied and checked for contamination.

If the situation is one occurring at a privately owned site but is of sufficient gravity that it will require the assistance of public agencies to control, the plan should take this into consideration as well. Planning should identify those agencies that may be called upon under certain emergency conditions, specify the types of assistance these agencies are capable of rendering, establish the methods by which they can be contacted for assistance, and identify those key individuals who are authorized to request such assistance as well as appropriate chains of command. Once the cooperation of public agency officials has been secured, meetings should be held during which frank discussions will outline potential problems that may be encountered by responding personnel. For example, if the emergency were to occur at a company that manufactures electrical cable or electrical power distribution equipment, certain hazardous substances may be present that, if they were exposed to high heat or flames, could release toxic fumes. At other facilities, certain dry chemical compounds will react violently if they come in contact with water. And a fire at certain nuclear facilities presents its own unique set of potential problems.

A detailed familiarization tour of the facility and potential problem areas is always a good idea. Generally this tour will result in a number of questions that should be responded to in as candid a manner as possible. It is recognized that there may be situations where, because of company proprietary processes or because of governmental security requirements, not all of the questions asked can be answered. In these situations, as much information as possible should be shared, using "generic" terms for proprietary processes whenever possible. When the information requested falls within the category of government classified, the inquirer should be courteously advised that this information cannot be provided. When it is felt that the information which is being withheld due to government security regulations may be essential to the proper provision of assistance, however, it is suggested that an arrangement be attempted whereby the company or agency ensures that there is a qualified individual available at all times who can interface with any emergency responders to ensure that proper safety issues are addressed and that the responders do not endanger themselves or the general public because of lack of necessary information. If possible, response commanders could be submitted for appropriate government clearance.

It is recommended that a listing of names and telephone numbers of all key personnel, be established. As changes occur, the lists should be updated and distributed. This, however, is not enough to ensure that a key change has not inadvertently been overlooked. To make contact lists truly meaningful, they should be reviewed on a monthly basis to ensure their viability. If there are no changes, nothing further need be done. When agreements have been made beforehand, the contact list should be periodically exercised. Such "exercising" should be routinely conducted as a prescheduled event, but on occasion, contact with no prior notice should be attempted, preferably at times such as weekends when personnel could be expected to be away from their normal contact numbers. In certain organizations, key personnel are equipped with wide-area personal pagers. Equipping key personnel with these devices almost guarantees that contact can be established when they are away from their normal contact phone numbers.

Assuming that a situation has occurred that requires assembling the CMT and again assuming that all members of the team have been contacted and directed to a prearranged location, what will they find when they get there? The ideal is to have a dedicated space available where the CMT will assemble. Such a space should provide ample working room; suitable emergency communications; all necessary supplies; and the capability of being fairly self-sustaining should commercial power fail, of being fairly near the scene of the problem (but not near enough to become unusable should the situation escalate), or of being located in a normal command center used by other governmental agencies such as fire and police), and of being reasonably accessible with the capability to control such access. In some organizations this is possible, but in the majority of the cases, the CMT will often find itself confined to make-shift quarters, which, more often than not, are either offices of senior members, or meeting rooms. If the choice of meeting spaces is open, then the selection of a meeting room is preferable, *provided* certain arrangements have been made in advance. For example, a small locked cabinet could be placed in the meeting room stocked with common items likely to be needed, such as paper or notepads, pens, pencils, blueprints, copies of operating procedural manuals, copies of the crisis mangement plan itself, lists of hazardous substances used at the affected facility, perhaps a base radio, and telephones. The meeting room should be equipped with a number of telephone jacks on several different telephone lines. The telephone handsets kept in the locked cabinet should be multiline sets that are capable of being switched to a single line should a conference call be required. If it is considered necessary, perhaps one or more of the phones can be equipped with a conference-call device (that is, speakerphone) where anyone in the room can participate in the call without having to use a handset. It may be desirable to have portable carrels available to give the members of the CMT who may be working at a common conference table some measure of privacy or at least to reduce the confusion caused when a great number of conversations are being carried on at one time. The availability of a base radio would enhance communications with front-line personnel who are engaged in on-scene handling of the situation (provided such communications are not being processed through an already established radio system such as might be found in an organization's maintenance or security departments). If radio communications will be handled directly from the Emergency Control Center (ECC), a suitable antenna with primary and back-up power systems should also be in place. The availability of restroom facilities close to the Emergency Control Center is certainly a big plus, as would be the availability of a stocked vending machine area or a kitchenette where food could be prepared if the situation is one of long duration. As previously mentioned, the location of the ECC should be one that provides easy, but controlled, access. The last thing the CMT will need, is to have the idle, the curious, the news media wandering in and out and interfering with attempts to control the situation. It may, in some cases, be necessary to post a guard at the entrance to the ECC to control such access. In a situation of this type, the person posted to control such access should have some means of identifying those persons who are authorized to enter. It is therefore suggested that an authorization card be prepared and issued to all members of the CMT and to any other key individuals who are designated as essential to any recovery operation. Such cards will allow access past control points and should be punched to accept a badge clip so that the card can be worn. The card should clearly identify the individual and preferably carry the individual's photo. This will require that cards be periodically reissued, but will also aid in preventing someone from gaining access to the ECC with an expired card. Another consideration, especially during these troubled times, is that a crisis or emergency situation may have been intentionally induced simply to cause the gathering of all key company or elected officials in one place at one time thereby making it easier for an adversary group to take hostages or to strike a potentially deadly blow to the organization by wiping out all leadership at once. While this possibility is more likely in the private sector, especially in cases involving news-sensitive companies (such as nuclear power plants, defense contractors, and petrochemical manufacturers) the possibility that such an event could occur and be directed specifically against elected officials should not be discounted. The potential for such actions increase when violence has occurred within the local community that may have involved certain ethnic, religious, or radical groups and that was successfully put down through the actions of local police, acting under the orders of the locally elected officials. Another possibility involves "retaliation" by certain fanatical elements within a community for actions against any group they may support, *anywhere else in the world*. The United States has experienced bombings in support of the anti-apartheid movement in South Africa, violence in support of Soviet Jewry, and a number of other, often symbolic, acts committed in support of, or protesting the actions of, governments in foreign lands. In many of these symbolic actions, nothing more violent than a large mass of people milling around in public, listening to speakers, and perhaps having a few of their number "symbolically" arrested will usually occur. In others, extensive property damage, injury, and even death have been the result. If the organization for which the planning is being conducted, could realistically find itself the target of terrorist actions, prudence should dictate that proper safety and security measures be taken to protect the leaders from just such an occurrence.

Some of the most common types of emergency likely to be faced involve situations that generally have some early warning signs. For example, acts of nature such as floods, hurricanes, and blizzards are usually predicted in advance of the actual event. The period following the prediction may also be short, however, such as cases involving tornados and earthquakes. In creating plans for dealing with natural-event emergencies, past history should serve as a guide. For example, while tornados have been recorded in every state, their incidence is much higher in the central and south-central United States than in the northeast or northwest United States. Therefore, planning for an emergency situation involving a tornado would be a very likely requirement for organizations within the zones or areas of greatest prevalence, but should not be totally discounted in those areas where the incidence of tornado activity is very low. In most cases, a weather radio, which will automatically begin broadcasting a weather alert when it is triggered by an electronic signal generated at the broadcast site, is certainly a good (and inexpensive) investment. In addition, if the organization has teletype facilities, detailed information may be obtained directly from the U.S. Weather Service whenever a weather-related emergency situation is developing. Arrangements for this service must be made in advance, however. When the organization is one in either industry or government that may be subject to adversarial actions, good intelligence reports are a *must!* Obviously, if the organization is not part of the federal government, it would, in all probability, not be possible to fund a formal intelligence network. If the organization is one involved in the defense industry, however, then a liaison with certain federal agencies that have access to intelligence data that could have an impact on the organization should be established and fostered. In nearly all cases, information received from such governmental agencies will be somewhat vague and will consist of actions that have take place elsewhere that could have repercussions on U.S. interests, and therefore organizations or individuals who feel they could be at risk should take appropriate measures to protect themselves or at least reduce their vulnerability. In some cases, where a specific target is known or a threat has been made by credible (and sometimes not so credible) sources, this information may also be passed along to risk groups/individuals/organizations. In maintaining a good liaison, it is essential that participating private entities or local governmental agencies share with the federal authorities intelligence information that may come into their possession regarding any adversarial groups regardless of their potential target interests. When the organization is of a type that could very likely be subject to adversarial actions, perhaps the best liaison to establish and maintain is one with local law enforcement officials. Once a good working relationship has been established, the information and assistance the police can render could well spell the difference between an "inconvenient" and a "disastrous" situation. During the planning phase, local police officials may well have some valuable input particularly in regard to the assistance they can provide. When preparing plans for meeting any emergency situation, it is not enough to assume that police assistance will automatically be provided when it is requested and in the quantity needed to meet the situation at hand *without prior contact and liaison!* All too often there is an attitude that, as a taxpayer, all that need be done is to make a call to the police and ask for their assistance and it will be provided. While the police *will* provide assistance without prior liaison, such assistance may not be adequate for the task, and by the time the situation is assessed by the police and properly responded to, major damage can have occurred and/or the situation can have escalated to the point where suppression and recovery operations may prove long and costly. To ensure that police officials have developed the proper appreciation for the potential problems at a facility, a detailed site tour is again recommended. Give the police site layout blueprints if they feel it will aid them in a proper response and if it is possible. These blueprints, however, should not be of such detail (particularly in regard to alarm systems) that, should they fall into the wrong hands, they could aid an adversary in gaining undetected site access.

Once the ECC has been established, news media personnel and all others who are not involved in addressing the emergency or crisis at hand must be kept under control. It is recommended that an area outside the ECC be set aside for representatives from the news media. Periodic briefings by an authorized spokesperson can take place in this area, and the entry/exit route to the ECC should not run through, or even close to, this news media briefing room. Personnel posted to control access to the ECC should be instructed that only authorized personnel, *in possession of proper credentials,* be allowed access. In cases where an individual's presence may be required in the ECC but that person does not have the necessary authorizing credentials he or she should be escorted the entire time they remain in the ECC. It is further recommended that a visitors' log or other similar record be maintained at the entrance to the ECC to record all necessary information on all such personnel entering the ECC. If the gravity of the situation dictates, consideration should be given to having all such visitor personnel and any hand-carried objects searched. Items that may be banned from the ECC include firearms, incendiary devices, cameras, unauthorized radios or transmitters, and tape recorders.

In many cases, especially in those involving the assembly of elected officials, an official car may be used to transport the individual to the ECC so that security of the parking area may not be a particular concern. In the private sector, or in those other areas where an official drives to the ECC, parking for personnel vehicles should be considered and should be in a secure area to prevent tampering with the vehicle for the purpose of harassment, implanting a listening device, taking a hostage, or even installing an explosive device. It is recommended that parking spots not be marked with names or titles of key personnel so as to provide no help in identifying a target's vehicle.

Recordkeeping within the ECC is an absolute must. The accurate recording of all information and data will provide a historical record of the event and may be used to critique all actions taken. Recording of this information should, whenever possible, be by electronic means. For example, a good tape recorder with omnidirectional microphone can be set up in the conference room to record all planning or decision-making meetings. Recording devices on all telephone lines will ensure that all information received can be retrieved if necessary and will document the instructions that may be issued. It may be desirable to install fixed closed circuit television (CCTV) cameras in the ECC that can record the presence of personnel during certain crucial decision-making periods. If all else fails, however, it can very well come down to one or more clerks manually recording essential data. If this is the case, it will be necessary to arrange for a pool of such personnel to be available to relieve these recorders periodically.

If electronic devices are used to provide the required records, it is important that someone be assigned to ensure that the recording media used in these devices is periodically removed, properly labeled, securely stored, and fresh recording media reinstalled. The individuals who may be making manual records should make careful note of the times of events, the names of the persons present, who-said-what-to-whom (if what was said directed a specific course of action), and each and every course of action. The recorders' names should be at the bottom of the record when they are relieved.

Finally, any "mutual aid" agreements or compacts with outside agencies, other facilities, or other recources should be documented in formal memoranda. Memoranda should be periodically reviewed and renewed, and the terms therein should be communicated to all appropriate personnel.

These are but a few of the elements essential to any plan. They have been discussed in an attempt to provide some insight into some of the areas that should be explored when plans to meet an emergency situation or crisis are being prepared.

8

Writing the Plan

Once the concept of preparing site or organization emergency plans is approved in principle, specific concurrence from the various department heads or staff managers, who have the responsibility and authority for directing the actions of persons or who may control certain assets or resources that may be used in support of certain aspects of the emergency plans, must be obtained. This concurrence and support must be unequivocal if the plans are to be meaningful and successful in their application. These department heads or staff managers must clearly understand that, while most incidents will be managed by the Crisis Management Team (CMT) composed of certain key officials, there may also be incidents that will place the responsibility for most, if not all, situational responses in the hands of one person who by virtue of his position or experience is the best person for the job at hand. In some cases, there may be reluctance by some members of the CMT to relinquish some of their authority, but for the good of the organization and the success of the plan, this must be factored in and planned for accordingly.

Actual preparation of *The Plan,* is not a matter to be rushed into. Only after careful and deliberate consideration and consultation with experts in certain specific areas if necessary, should plan preparation commence. In some instances, especially in an industry where federal, state, or local agencies may exercise regulatory authority over site operation, certain exemptions from requirements may have to be requested. This should be done as early in the planning process as possible. Any exemptions requested must be clearly stated showing reasons for such requests, the limited conditions under which the deviation(s) from established requirements will occur, and the measures that will be used (when or where applicable) to compensate for the deviation(s).

One of the best approaches to plan preparation involves the drafting of a preliminary outline that lists the threats or emergency conditions with which the plan will prepare the organization to deal. After the outline has been reviewed by the appropriate management-level personnel, and refined as necessary, the details of *each* plan will be added, progressing in a logical manner through a natural escalation process from the lowest threat or emergency condition level through its severest levels and beyond to the post-incident level where specific actions must be taken to initiate a resumption of normal operations.

As an example of the type of thinking involved or questions that must be resolved in preparing an emergency plan, the following deals with preparing a plan or procedure for a bomb threat:

Preliminary Preparation

1. Which staff manager or other member of the CMT will have primary responsibility for controlling the organization's response?
2. What, if any, are the limits on this persons' authority/responsibility in responding?
3. What resources are available to support the organization's response?
   a. personnel (trained, volunteer search teams)
   b. portable radios (must be controlled to avoid electromagnetic detonation)
   c. portable explosives detectors (available to check suspicious objects)
   d. trained dogs (may be available from local law enforcement agencies when time is not limited)
   e. in-house fire department (or immediate availability of municipal fire department personnel and equipment for standby in case of actual explosion and fire (fire department personnel should *not* be used to search for a bomb)
   f. bomb blanket, bomb basket, and bags, and so forth (shield, not cover, suspect objects to minimize blast damage)
   g. emergency lights
   h. detailed facility plans/blueprints
   i. listening devices (stethoscope or electronic sound amplification device to check suspicious objects)
   j. automatic telephone recording devices
   k. established evacuation plan in which personnel are periodically exercised
   l. plant/building emergency notification system
   m. designated and equipped emergency command center
   n. medical personnel and/or trained medical technicians (EMTs)/ medical response technicians (MRTs)

While no *single* plan is applicable to *every* facility, a good generic plan can be modified to meet specific site requirements. Such a plan has been prepared by the U.S. Department of the Treasury, Bureau of Alcohol, Tobacco, and Firearms, and is reprinted in its entirety in Appendix F.

As can be seen, the generic plan offered by the Bureau of Alcohol, Tobacco, and Firearms, provides an excellent planning base from which any organization can obtain the necessary basic data for preparing its individually unique Bomb Threat Plan.

A number of "generic" guides are offered by the Federal Emergency Management Administration (FEMA) (see Appendix G).

9

Coordinating and Testing the Plan

Finally, FINALLY!!!, we have a plan. Without coordinating the plan with all personnel and/or agencies who will be involved in its implementation, however, it might as well sit in a desk drawer forever because, if it is ever needed, it will be needed quickly and *that* is not the time to be contacting individuals and telling them what is expected of them.

Ideally, everyone who will ultimately have a position of responsibility in implementing the plan, will have had significant input into the plan's preparation. This initial input, however, cannot be construed as providing the individual with the intimate knowledge necessary to make the plan work successfully. Nor would the individual be completely familiar with those whom he or she would be interacting, the finite details of assigned responsibilities, or the lines of authority and command.

After all the minute details have been hammered out and after receiving the concurrence of all individuals and/or agencies who will be involved in the plan's implementation, it should be published in sufficient quantities to ensure that a copy is available to everyone who has been assigned responsibilities therein. If the plan divulges certain vulnerabilities that the governing authority does not wish to become generally known, the plan should perhaps be written in such a manner that all sensitive information can be contained within a single supplement that will have limited distribution.

Because other individuals or support groups who may not have a directly assigned responsibility in the plan will be required to perform in a certain manner, it will be the responsibility of the middle-level managers and supervisors who have been delegated certain specific responsibilities to communicate to those individuals under their control or command the duties they will be expected to perform and possibly to include additional details such as emergency assembly instructions, evacuation instructions, location of specialized equipment and supplies, and reporting responsibilities—perhaps even spelling these duties out in great detail.

If the plan will require the services of local law enforcement personnel in effecting total implementation, the plan should carry a clearly worded memorandum of understanding (approved by the senior police offical of the agency providing assistance) that spells out the services that will be rendered in an emergency, the number of police who will be detailed to provide such assistance, and the amount of time it will take for their arrival at the scene of the emergency after they have been notified.

If the emergency that the plan has been formulated to address is one in which existing weather conditions may play a significant role, prior contact with the National Weather Service or a qualified local meteorologist should be established and documented in the plan if possible. If the facility has access to the appropriate equipment, arrangements may be made with a weather service to obtain periodic weather alert bulletins.

Upon completion of the final draft of any plan, it should be reviewed by all parties who may be required to perform or provide support services in accordance with its provisions. These independent reviews will, in all probability, result in further modifications; however, the resulting rewritten plan should be in its final form. If, during this final draft review process, substantial changes are made by any persons, all parties should have the opportunity to review such changes since they may impact on their portion of the plan and require negotiation between the departments or agencies involved.

Once the plan has been finalized and signed by all involved parties or written commitment to the provision of certain essential support services received from outside agencies, it must be quickly and clearly communicated to all affected personnel including employees who will be charged with carrying out its provisions. If the plan is detailed, it may be advisable to conduct a formal training session to explain its requirements and to answer the inevitable questions that will result.

After the plan has been finalized and communicated to all affected personnel, it must be tested and exercised to determine under reasonably controlled conditions if it is practical and workable. Initially, exercises should be conducted involving only key personnel. As these personnel become intimately familiar with plan requirements, the scope of participation may be expanded until drills and exercises can be conducted that involve all persons who would be used in dealing with the actual emergency. While the majority of the exercises may be simply a *walk-through* to test each person's understanding of the plan requirements and to test equipment, there should also be a major unannounced exercise at least once a year. Planning for this exercise must be carried out in relative secrecy in order to test meaningfully a number of plan requirements including the ability to contact key personnel outside of normal working hours, the ability for personnel contacted to quickly respond, the availability of necessary equipment and supplies in adequate amounts, and even the decision-making abilities of certain key personnel.

During other periods of the year, various independent departments or agencies may wish to conduct their own exercises to test their individual abilities to respond and to provide the necessary services. These exercises, while limited in scope, play a very important part in ensuring that each element is capable and ready to respond in the expected manner at all times.

During the major unannounced exercise recommended above, it is believed valuable information can be obtained by assigning any number of recorders to follow key personnel and/or key response elements to videotape, in documentary style, their performance. These videotapes can later be reviewed by appropriate personnel to enable them to critique their own performance. Based on the evaluation of the results obtained from the exercise and a review of the videotapes made, necessary modifications may be made in the plan to meet the desired objectives.

10

Emergency Plan Considerations

Planning for an emergency can greatly tax available resources both at the planning and implementation stages. This is especially true in smaller communities where many of these responsibilities come under state or county control or where it is often the task of volunteers to prepare and carry out such plans. All too often, unexercised prepared plans may be found wanting when they must be quickly placed into effect. Unfortunately, it seems to be human nature to devote little time and energy to preparing for something that may never happen. This is not necessarily a bad thing provided an intelligent evaluation has been made of the potential for an incident of a particular type to occur and a conscientious decision has been made that the probability factor is very low. In these cases, less planning and preparation will be necessary. In many cases, one situation can be responded to by an emergency plan prepared for an altogether different situation.

Perhaps the most common type of incident in the public sector, one where great numbers of citizens are simultaneously affected by a single event, involves an accident where hazardous chemicals are released into the environment. This has become an all-too-frequent occurrence in some rural sections of the country where railroad accidents involving tank cars filled with bulk chemicals have derailed with serious and potentially deadly effects. It is not uncommon to see television newsfilm of train wrecks in which a tangled jumble of railroad cars are burning fiercely with great clouds of toxic gases and smoke billowing into the atmosphere. The narrative accompanying this dramatic news footage will be something like "Residents were hastily evacuated—some escaped in only their night clothes." This often terse statement fails miserably in conveying the shock, upheaval, and loss being experienced by the evacuees. It also fails to convey the sudden and possibly continuing need for community support services. In most cases, those persons removed from the danger zone are sheltered in community schools or churches. Where good emergency plans have been prepared beforehand, these emergency shelters are stocked with certain items beyond the requisite food and blankets, items which provide some small measure of comfort and preserve personal dignity to those being sheltered. For example, in addition

45

to the basic food and blankets, cots or air mattresses would certainly be appreciated by those who may have to spend more than a few hours away from their homes. Other considerations could include some means of dividing large open floor spaces (such as exist in gymnasiums) into smaller cubicles in which families could enjoy some small measure of privacy in long-term situations.

Health and comfort items such as toothbrushes, toothpaste, toilet soap, and even sanitary napkins might be welcome to those who did not have time to acquire them before leaving their homes. A dispensary where common nonprescription medicines and first aid supplies such as aspirin, cough syrup, Bandaids®, and antiseptic are available should be considered. If a medical facility is not near the shelter, an area where medical personnel could set up an emergency aid station, should be predesignated and stocked with basic supplies.

When it appears that the persons who have been evacuated from the danger zone may be away from their homes for a long period of time, the availability of telephones with which they can contact friends and relatives to reassure them of their safety would ease their minds and would probably result in far fewer telephone calls to local officials from these same friends and relatives who are fearful or concerned for the health and safety of their friends and relations. In those situations where the American Red Cross has the capabilities, many of these "extras" may indeed be provided. If the emergency were to occur in a rural area, however, some distance from Red Cross assistance, such assistance could take some time to arrive particularly if all normal access routes are impassable.

In some cases, people bring pets with them to emergency shelters. What special accommodations can be made for these animals? It is not an especially good idea to have animals crowded into a confined space with a great number of unfamiliar humans. It is unfair to those who may be allergic to animals or who may fear them; animals who are not confined could end up fighting and injuring themselves or humans who try to interfere; sanitation could be affected, and so forth. When the evacuees have provided their own transportation to the shelter, the obvious choice is to have the pets remain in the personal vehicle. Another consideration may be to restrict those with animals to certain rooms in the shelter or even further to provide space(s) within the shelter where pets could be properly housed away from the general population. In some areas, this will not be an item of major concern; yet in others such as retirement communities where elderly persons have great affection for their pets it should be seriously considered as it is a problem likely to be encountered.

In today's age of smokers versus nonsmokers rights, consideration should be given to banning smoking inside the shelter or to designating smoking areas away from the general shelter population.

If the means are available, secure storage of small valuables such as jewelry or cash in a continuously manned location, might be considered.

One-time-use envelopes are available in which the valuables can be placed. The owner can record his name, address, and other pertinent information on the outside of the envelope and be given a claim check corresponding to the number on the envelope. Use of the one-time-use envelope will ensure that the envelope has not been tampered with once it leaves the owner's control as any attempt to do so will be quickly revealed. It is imperative that these valuables be locked away in a *continuously* manned post to ensure against further catastrophic loss. A notice should be posted announcing that the acceptance of the valuables for storage imposes no liability for their loss on the cognizant civil authorities or individuals accepting the items for storage. A separate form (waiver) which the individual requesting secure storage would sign, is also desirable. Such storage repository should be substantial and adequately anchored, and access to its contents should be restricted, taking two authorized individuals to open the container—neither one posted in the continuously manned post in which it is located.

Frequent news of the status of the emergency condition that caused their assembly in the shelter should be made known to all individuals. There are two means by which this can be accomplished—either a bulletin board posting or a public address system announcement. Unless the news is life threatening, public address announcements should be restricted. Bulletin board notices should be consistent in format and location and should be written large enough to be seen and read by those with bad eyesight. Two by three foot newsprint is an ideal medium for this purpose.

If possible, able-bodied individuals should be offered the opportunity to aid in meeting the crisis. For example, in a flood situation, most men and teenagers will be eager to volunteer to help build sandbag dikes. This serves a number of purposes—it obviously helps to fight the problem, gives the participating individuals a sense of purpose and control in an otherwise uncontrollable situation, helps them to think of something other than their personal problems, and helps to develop a spirit of cooperation that may very well stay with them long after the emergency is over. For those left behind in the shelter, it is also important that they be offered the opportunity to participate in some meaningful way in meeting the crisis at hand. If the situation revolves around a flood, perhaps the preparation of new sand bags from stocks of raw material can be organized; others can help in food preparation, shelter clean-up, nursery care, and organizing and conducting games for the small children.

If there is a professional photographer (or a good amateur one) among the shelter population and the equipment and supplies are available or procurable, consideration might be given to making this individual the official chronicler of the entire situation. Action scenes of citizens working to overcome the crisis along with less dramatic shots of daily shelter life would be welcome in the municipalities' archives as a record of the community's travail and of their efforts in overcoming it and, indeed, could become momentos of hard times shared and battles fought and won.

Planners must address the emotional side of an emergency. Emotions might run high. People might be less tolerant of each other and the responses being made to the event—"It's taking too long!" or "We're not being told anything!" If possible, a psychologist or psychiatrist should be incorporated into the planning phase and, should an event occur, his or her services should be used. Regardless of how, the emotional issues of displaced persons will have to be addressed.

Stocks of some type of universal-fit clothing should either be available in the shelter or close by. For example, in those cases where individuals were not able to dress properly themselves when leaving their homes, suitable clothing should be provided. This may be nothing more than a disposable Tyvek® jumpsuit with one or more blankets substituting for coats. The problem of adequate footwear can be similarly addressed by using disposable slippers similar to those provided at many hospitals. These are adequate for indoor wear and are durable enough for several days wear.

During the initial planning stages, consideration might be given to any special dietary needs that could become an issue should a large number of local residents suddenly have to occupy the shelter. This may require a survey of those who might become temporary shelter residents to ascertain if they have any special needs based upon medical or religious necessity. If the number of respondents justifies taking this into consideration, then plans should include provisions for this if possible. In these cases, it may be necessary to stagger feeding periods so that food preparation facilities can be used to feed the general shelter population separately from those with special dietary requirements.

If the emergency is one in which all overland access routes have become impassable (such as in the case of a flood), has consideration been given to establishing a helicopter landing pad? It may be necessary to evacuate injured persons by air and to bring supplies such as empty sand bags and generator fuel into the emergency shelter. Helicopter support may be the only means by which this can be accomplished. In establishing a helicopter landing zone, site it away from occupied buildings and in an area where there are no power lines or poles, trees, radio towers, and so forth close by that can present hazards for the helicopter crew. When a landing zone has been established and all hazards such as trees and power poles have been identified, a map should be prepared showing as accurately as possible the locations of all such hazards and distances from the landing zone to them. This map should be distributed to all agencies from which it is anticipated aircraft assistance might be provided. The landing site should be paved and painted with the appropriate symbol, which can be easily recognized from the air. For night operations, it would be useful if floodlights, located at a safe distance from the landing zone, were available. It is important that any floodlights installed for the purpose of nighttime helicopter operations be positioned in such a fashion that they not shine into the aircraft pilot's eyes during landing operations and so that no obstacle that poses a hazard to aircraft lies within their area of illumination. In addition, there should be vehicular access to the landing area to allow an ambulance or other vehicle to deliver a patient to the evacuation helicopter quickly or a truck or other vehicle picking up emergency supplies to move as close as possible to cut down the amount of time in receiving the delivered items. For day and night helicopter operations, there should be firefighting apparatus immediately available with personnel trained and equipped to deal with an aircraft accident. The landing area should be checked periodically and any litter or refuse immediately cleaned up since any piece of debris could be ingested into a turbine engine on landing or takeoff. If this should happen, it could at the very least, cause considerable damage to the aircraft, and in the worse case, it could cause a crash. In addition, "rotor-wash" could propel loose objects on the ground causing a hazard. Depending upon the agency to which the helicopter is assigned, there should be a means of communicating with the aircraft at all times. For example, if the helicopter is provided by a police department, communication between it and a police patrol vehicle on the ground may satisfy this requirement. If the helicopter belongs to a branch of the military, some prior special arrangements may have to be made to ensure that two-way conversation during any emergency can be established and maintained. Communication is necessary, for instance, because the pilot may need necessary information such as surface wind speed and direction if this information is not readily apparent such as during conditions of restricted visibility. In addition, the pilot can request that the landing area floodlights be activated, give his estimated time of arrival in order to allow the firefighting crew to get in position, and so forth.

In any situation in which it appears that area residents may have to evacuate their homes quickly, vehicle fuel tanks should be kept as full as possible. A tanker truck could be used to do this. (Even fuel tanks in disabled vehicles should be kept full.) This serves a two-fold purpose. First, it ensures that the vehicle will be ready to roll at a moment's notice. In some situations there may not be a great deal of advance notice, and the evacuation may require driving a long distance. The second reason for keeping fuel tanks as full as possible, even those in disabled vehicles, becomes apparent upon arrival at the emergency shelter. At this time, whatever fuel remains in vehicle tanks can become a reservoir from which emergency vehicles such as trucks, ambulances, fire apparatus, and police vehicles may be refueled should normal supplies be cut off. In addition, if the shelter is provided with a gasoline-powered generator or if small portable gasoline-powered generators are available to power pumps or provide electricity for emergency lights, the fuel in vehicle tanks is a readily available resource. Portable emergency generators can usually operate on either leaded or unleaded gasoline. Great care must be taken, however, to ensure that diesel fuel is not inadvertently placed into a gasoline-powered model or, perhaps more importantly, that gasoline is not introduced into a diesel-powered engine. These types of mistakes could occur when personnel are fatigued or when volunteers are not familiar with the requirements of the various types of engines. Should the wrong fuel be used, a vital piece of equipment can be lost and the consequences are potentially disastrous.

In certain types of emergencies such as a flood, there is usually a warning period during which personnel can prepare. In those areas where periodic widespread flooding is a fact of life, consideration should be given to identifying those persons who own boats that could be used in the evacuation of personnel from flooded areas and in patroling residential areas during the emergency to prevent looting. These persons would obviously have to volunteer their equipment, and depending on the resources of the community, may or may not be reimbursed for their damages or losses incurred as the result of their involvement in the emergency operations. Depending on the state, either the Department of Motor Vehicles or the Environmental Protection/ Fish & Game Agency are charged with the responsibility for registration of all boats of over a certain length. Contact with the appropriate state agency (by appropriate authorities) should result in a list of names of all local boat owners with brief description of their boats. This in turn may be used in a mailing or telephone call campaign explaining what is desired and soliciting their cooperation. Those persons choosing to participate should be instructed that, when they are notified that their watercraft will be needed, they should bring them with all fuel tanks filled to a safe, predesignated staging area. Note that once the staging area has been designated and boats are positioned there, some sort of security must be provided to prevent theft or vandalism since, sadly, there are some unthinking or uncaring individuals who will see this as an opportunity for personal gain rather than as a selfless service to the entire community. The boats should carry all normal safety equipment such as life jackets, anchor and rope and a pump. Extra rope, if available, should also be carried as it may be required in evacuating persons from flooded areas. During nighttime operations, a high intensity, portable floodlight will also be extremely valuable. Since boats will be operating in waters of uncertain depth, filled with all sorts of debris, safety shrouds to protect motor propellors should be considered. This could help to prevent a rescuer from becoming a rescuee. Persons who have volunteered their time and equipment to aid the community, should be called together on a periodic basis and given some training that emphasizes things like avoiding roiled or very fast moving water, being constantly on the alert for large pieces of debris in the crosscurrents which could capsize the boat, staying away from power lines in the water, not smoking (in case they are in the vicinity of a broken gas line), and approaching all persons in the water from downstream or against the current or throwing them a rope and pulling them to the boat. Large domestic or wild animals such as deer, cows, and horses can be rescued, but it is a dangerous situation. In these cases, the animal should be tethered to the side of the boat, ensuring that a leg or tail cannot come in contact with the engine propellor, then the boat should be slowly maneuvered toward high ground. The boat operator should be aware that the person holding the tether must be ready to release it instantly, for as soon as the animal feels solid footing beneath it, it may begin thrashing about and will have to be released to reach high ground on its own or else risk injury or damage to the boat, its occupants, and even the rescued animal. In areas where snakes are prevalent, they will be found in the water and in nearly any object, natural or manmade, that is above the high-water mark and that affords them some refuge. Most snakes are nonpoisonous, but in the generally flood-prone areas, rattlers, water moccasins, and copperheads may be found. Personnel should be cautioned to look before reaching into, over, or around any object in the water. Personnel manning the boats should be cautioned against wearing chest waders or hip boots in the boats. If the boat were to suddenly overturn in deep water, the waders could flip the wearer upside down and keep him or her underneath until he or she drowns. Hip boots on the other hand, will simply fill with water and drag the person to the bottom—not an especially appealing choice in either case. Sneakers or loose fitting footwear that can be quickly kicked off in this type of emergency are recommended. The use of inflatable boats is not especially recommended due to the constant danger of their being punctured and thereby endangering the occupants.

In certain small communities, it is probably a natural assumption that the senior civil official will automatically assume control in the event of any emergency or catastrophic situation. If, however, there is an individual who is responsible for civil defense and who has received necessary training, he or she might be a better choice for designation as the person in charge. Such delegation of responsibility is the prerogative of the local civil authorities but should be decided beforehand and formalized with clearly defined lines of responsibility and communication as well as limits of authority. If the severity of the situation or the demographic and/or logistical considerations are such that one individual cannot exercise effective control, then whichever official is predesignated to assume control, should be assigned assistants. Similar preassignment of the assistants before an incident, rather than their ad hoc selection from volunteers at the emergency evacuation center, will substantially reduce the number of false starts and wasted efforts that occur in situations where personnel are asked to perform in unfamiliar ways and in unfamiliar circumstances.

If there is a hospital or other health care facility such as a nursing home or a sanatorium located within an emergency evacuation area, a different set of problems will be encountered that will require considerations to be made and solutions to be developed. Can the person who has the authority to initiate an evacuation at the affected facility be reached at all hours? Is there an adequate number of ambulances or other specialized vehicles available to transport those patients or individuals who, due to illness, injury, or infirmity, require special transport? Are these ambulances/specialized vehicles immediately available at the health care facility, or must they be called in from private agencies and/or municipal public service departments? Is there a method in place to initiate pooling of these vehicles and attendant personnel with a minimum number of phone calls? For those patients who are ambulatory, have alternative means of transport such as public buses been provided, and what means are in place to ensure their quick provision? Will these evacuees be relocated in another health care facility, or will they be temporarily housed in some sort of emergency shelter due to the unavailability of any other suitable alternative? If they are relocated to an emergency shelter located in a public building or church, have adequate stocks of medical supplies and medication been brought from the evacuated facility to maintain health services until the individuals can be transferred to a proper facility, or conversely, has an alternative source of supply such as a well-stocked pharmacy been predesignated? If it is not possible to transfer patients to a proper health care facility and accommodations must be improvised, laundry facilities become very important. If the emergency shelter is a school and the school is large and has an athletic department, washing machines and clothes dryers may already be present. These can be used for cleaning bed linens evacuated with the patients. If this type of arrangement is available in the shelter, it is recommended that arrangements be made with the hospital, nursing home, or other facility to deliver an adequate reserve stock of bed linens to the shelter before, or in conjunction with, the arrival of patients.

Another major concern is an adequate supply of potable water. In many rural communities, drilled wells are the most common source of water with each building having its own well. If the emergency shelter is provided with a private well, consideration should be given to installation of some type of commercially available water filtration and/or treatment system into the supply line to all faucets. In the event that the water supply becomes contaminated as a result of the situation that caused the emergency condition to be declared, a filtration/treatment system could prove to be a major blessing. If such a system is not available, potable water may still be possible by boiling or batch treating it with chlorine bleach. When the possibility exists that the water supply could be contaminated, some method of frequent checks should be established and conducted by qualified personnel to ensure that the water being used in the shelter is safe. If the water must be treated with chlorine, powdered fruit-flavored drink concentrates can serve to make it more palatable, though these should be served as cold as possible as this diminishes most objectionable tastes. In addition, such preparations may contain sugar and may, therefore, have to be avoided by some people.

Yet another area of concern when dealing with emergencies is crowd control. It is a natural thing for people to congregate at the scene of an extraordinary occurrence. Since it is such a natural thing, planning should incorporate the phenomenon so that an appropriate response can be generated. Depending on the nature of the emergency and its scope and/or location, methods for dealing with groups of onlookers will vary. Again, the emotional aspect must be considered. What an individual may feel may be exacerbated by a crowd. Many times a collective mentality will be manifested by a crowd.

Those responsible for maintaining order must recognize that controlling groups of people is not so much a physical issue as it is a psychological one. It has been said that in a prison riot situation authorities have about thirty minutes to quell the uprising before a "leader" emerges to take charge of the group. This is also the case with emotionally charged spectators. After a short while, certain personalities may emerge and take over the crowd. Depending on circumstances and the emergent personality, this may be good or bad. If the emergency, by its nature, precludes emotion or concentrates it in such a way that the crowd is not affected, crowd control will for the most part involve keeping people away from hazardous situations or keeping access or rescue routes clear. It is not uncommon for people to want to lend a hand. If crowd members are willing and can be used as volunteer rescue workers, a source of manpower can be tapped. Others can be pressed into service to assist "official" authorities with rescue-related functions.

One important job often overlooked during planning for an emergency is that of ground guide(s). Whenever a fire department is summoned to a large manufacturing facility, for example, how many times is a security officer or someone else dispatched to the closest landmark to meet responding fire apparatus and guide it to the exact location where it is needed? Large manufacturing complexes or, for that matter, retail complexes such as malls contain many different and varied facilities some of which are more prone to emergencies than others. Unless firefighters are intimately familiar with all such facilities within their jurisdiction (or, in the case of mutual-aid compacts, areas outside of their jurisdiction), valuable time will be lost while responders try to find exact locations where their services are required. Crowd members can be effectively used for this purpose thus providing a valuable contribution to the overall effort.

Considerations when developing emergency plans are numerous, complex, and varied. No one individual can be expected to think of all the things necessary to a successful response to an emergency event. It is imperative that group interaction take place during planning so the multitude of things that must be considered are addressed. It is *always* smarter to have something and not need it than to need something and not have it.

Many emergencies that may affect a great number of local residents or employers will not require a mass evacuation of persons to a central assembly point. Examples include a massive and prolonged power outage, a blizzard, an earthquake, a bridge collapse, or even the release or spill of a hazardous or toxic substance.

Many public water supplies, that is, reservoirs, are located adjacent to highways. This holds the potential for an extremely serious problem should a vehicle accident result in one or more automobiles or trucks ending up in the water. The contamination caused by spilled fuel could, in all probability, take a number of days to clear up. During this period, it may be possible for the responsible municipality to tap into alternative or backup reservoirs or wells to provide at least a limited flow of potable water to affected households. Also during this period (especially if an alternative supply is limited), it may be necessary to impose water restrictions by mandating hours of use, requiring high-water-use industries to shut down, or even resorting to allowing water to flow into the system for limited periods of time each day, that is, controlled rationing (thought must be given in this case to the effect on firefighting ability). It might even be necessary to request assistance from an appropriate source such as the National Guard to ferry in clean water in tankers, commonly referred to as "Water Buffalos, or simply "Buffalos." Once it is decided that the fuel spill has been adequately cleaned up or diluted to the point that it is no longer dangerous to the public, it may be necessary to flush all the water lines to remove any residue, and it may well require treatment of the water at the filtration plant or pumping station. All of this will cause hardships (to varying degrees) on great numbers of people, but it cannot be considered a catastrophic event since the system will be back in operation fairly quickly.

Imagine, however, if the vehicle (or vehicles) involved in an accident that caused them to either end up in the water supply or caused their cargos to be discharged into the water supply were tractor trailers (or freight cars), carrying bulk cargo either tankers carrying toxic chemicals or dry cargo that could react with water such as chlorine. Depending on the material, a mass evacuation of the surrounding area might or might not be required. In either case, an immediate cessation of water pumping activities from this reservoir, should take place. Steps would have to be taken to remove the vehicle(s) from the water as quickly as possible to reduce the amount of material discharged or to otherwise contain material that might reach the water from a nearby accident scene. In a removal operation, the services of specialized equipment may be necessary. Depending on the size of the vehicle and whether it has to be lifted from the water or can be pulled back up onto solid ground, one or more large vehicles designed for towing of tractor trailers or buses, may be required. It may be necessary to arrange for the services of a heavy lift crane. Because there are many parts of the country where such recovery vehicles or equipment are not readily available, consideration should be given to planning for such a possibility by locating the types of equipment that could be required, making arrangements with the owner(s) for their quick deployment, and identifying access routes to the scenes of any potential emergency situation, routes that do not require the vehicles to pass over bridges that might not be able to carry their weight, under overpasses where they could be blocked from further progress, or over roads that cannot support their weight, are not wide enough to permit safe passage, or have a number of sharp turns that would not allow necessary maneuvering. If the removal operation will be one of long duration, it may be desirable to begin removal of the hazardous material (if liquid) from a partially submerged vehicle as soon as leakage is detected. In this case, a suitable storage vessel(s) and necessary pumps and hoses would have to be quickly provided. Depending on the nature of the pollutant (for example, a corrosive) special hoses and pumps as well as a suitable receiving tank may be required. In this case, all personnel involved in the operation would in all likelihood be required to wear protective clothing and breathing apparatus such as air packs. Again if these personnel will be involved in a lengthy situation, arrangements must be made to maintain a steady supply of fresh air-pack tanks. It would be advisable to have an ambulance and EMTs/MRTs standing by, police to control the curious and keep them far enough away so that they do not inadvertently enter any danger zone, a spokesman who can interface with the news media, and area floodlighting if the operation occurs in, or will continue into, the hours of darkness.

If an accident occurred near a reservoir but all vehicles involved remained on dry land and only leakage into the water supply is occurring, efforts to contain this leak and prevent it from entering any drainage systems or leaching into the water supply must be initiated as quickly as possible. Efforts could include polyethylene sheeting and earthen dams with trash pumps used to suction the collected material (if it is liquid) into appropriate containers. Use of pumps designed to operate in debris-choked environments will ensure that containment and clean-up operations can continue and need not stop because of mechanical breakdown. If the material is a solid, clean-up may be much easier, requiring a bucket loader and/or clean-up brigade of people with brooms and shovels. In these scenarios, however, the *assumption* is made that the material would be hazardous if let loose into the environment (including the air); therefore clean-up may not be something that should be assigned to a highway or road maintenance crew. The clean-up may require a great deal of specialized equipment and the expertise of the operators of this equipment. There are companies that specialize in operations of this type. Unfortunately, if such an incident were to occur in an area located some distance from such a clean-up company, it might take a long time for professional assistance to arrive. In this case, containment and/or clean-up operations may very well fall to the local fire department. Most fire departments, even those composed of volunteers, usually have had some training in dealing with hazardous or toxic substances. Where such training and/or expertise is available, cleanup operations, possibly in conjunction with highway maintenance personnel, may have to be initiated in order to prevent further damage. Any such attempts should, of course, be predicated on the assumption that adequate safety measures are taken and that necessary protective equipment is available and used to protect against an accurately identified hazard. In some cases, federal assistance by the National Guard may be directed.

11

Recovery

With few exceptions, there will usually be some warning signs present that will alert any organization to the possible need to implement emergency plans. The organization should incorporate into the plans, a designated group capable of recognizing the early warning signs. This group should have the ability to be quickly detached from other duties and assigned exclusively to situational monitoring. This group assembled in the Emergency Control Center (ECC) should have the responsibility and authority to initiate contact with the Crisis Management Team (CMT) and may carry out certain actions directed by the CMT prior to their arrival on site or their assumption of control, actions such as calling in certain key individuals, contacting supporting groups or external agencies, shutting down of processes, preparing equipment; acquiring supplies.

Once the CMT arrives onsite or assumes control of the situation, the personnel who have been manning the ECC can serve as advisers to the CMT and implement their decisions. This will require that their authority and lines of command be clearly delineated in the plan.

As an addendum to any plan, a current call-in list of all key personnel must be maintained as well as the emergency contact numbers for outside support groups. These support groups should be alerted if possible when it appears that a situation may be developing that might require their participation. This simple courtesy will allow them to prepare accordingly and will result in a speedier and better organized response.

If it appears that implementation of an emergency plan will impact employees who are not directly involved in such implementation, these personnel should be briefed or at least advised of what is occurring and their responsibilities should be explained.

If the developing situation is one in which certain preparations must be made beforehand such as in the case of an approaching hurricane, some personnel will play a larger role than will others in preparing for the event. The maintenance staff should be detached from all other responsibilities and augmented as necessary by additional personnel to ensure that the fuel tanks of all vehicles are full, fuel supplies for emergency generators are adequate, all large windows are protected from wind and flying objects, all items that may be stored out of doors and that could become flying hazards during a hurricane are properly tied down or stored indoors, chain saws and other appropriate items are available if clearing downed trees becomes necessary, and volunteer personnel are identified who will remain at the facility throughout the storm. These volunteers should be listed by their individual specialties such as electrician, welder, or plumber.

To ensure some measure of comfort to those personnel who will be remaining onsite during the course of the emergency, there should be an adequate stock of food and if necessary cots and bedding. Other emergency supplies include flashlights with a generous supply of fresh batteries, stocks of plywood and other materials that may be used to cover windows and doors broken by the wind, and video or still cameras and film to record damage for insurance claim purposes.

The plan should not be written so rigidly that it does not allow for some modification to meet existing circumstances as all too often in these situations Murphy's Law will come into play whenever the opportunity presents itself.

As a means of ensuring that everything possible has been done to meet the impending situation, detailed checklists should be developed and used. In developing these checklists, the adage, "Better to have it and not need it than to need it and not have it," should be kept in mind. The middle of a hurricane is not the time to discover that you have run out of toilet paper!

An emergency plan for dealing with a hurricane can be found in Appendix B.

In the event of a catastrophic event in which senior and/or key members of the organization may lose their lives or be so severely injured that their services would be lost for extended periods of time, it is crucial to the organization's continued viability that there be other personnel who may be nearly as well qualified who can step in and ensure continued operations. The best method for guaranteeing the availability of a qualified replacement, is to require that each senior official and/or key member of the organization, train a subordinate to assume the higher position. This will serve a two-fold purpose: First, it ensures that necessary organizational operations or the organization's mission can be carried out despite the loss (permanent or temporary) of key personnel, and second, it provides some incentive for junior personnel to excel in their performance and seek advancement within the organization. It should be recognized, however, that people will be people, and there will probably be some individuals who feel they are indispensable to the organization and who will fail to train a subordinate either because of a fear that they will be ousted by this person or because they feel that the subordinate will never be capable of meeting their performance standards. It is, therefore, the responsibility of the board of directors to ensure the personnel backup system is in place and ready to be implemented when it becomes necessary.

While we are on the subject of backup systems, it is prudent to provide some sort of backup system for vital records. Many companies now store copies of records on microfilm or other recording medium in safe locations away from the main site. In this way, return to normal operations can be accelerated in the event of a catastrophic loss of the physical plant or an electronic records system.

In returning a facility to normal operation after any sort of serious damage or incident, it is probable that not all plant or organizational employees will be necessary, at least in the initial and early stages of recovery. It would, therefore, benefit any organization to identify those individuals who possess noncritical skills and who would be furloughed until recovery operations have progressed to a point where normal operations can be resumed. Some organizations might find it beneficial to plan for a phased recall of personnel; others might want to wait until full and unhindered operations can be resumed. In either case, it is important that personnel contact addresses and telephone numbers be accurate and up to date. It might also benefit the organization to send out a recovery operations briefing sheet or bulletin periodically to those personnel who have been furloughed telling them what is being done to return operations to normal and how the recovery process is progressing. This will make them feel that they are still a valued part of the organization.

In the event of a situation in which a great deal of damage is incurred and/or in which injuries result, there will probably be legal issues raised and perhaps some involving liability. It would be in the best interest of any organization to be proactive in this area and to have legal counsel's input during plan preparation and some assurance that such counsel can be quickly contacted if needed. To assist in either the defense of the organization or in any civil or criminal actions the organization may seek to pursue, it is imperative that clear, concise, and accurate records of all that led up to the emergency, what transpired during the emergency, and what took place after the emergency be maintained. These records, when they are documented by date, time, complete descriptions of events, names of persons involved, names of witnesses, and so forth will be very important in the construction of an after-action report. This report should be as detailed as possible and should contain statements from personnel, photographs, and even physical evidence if that is considered necessary. In the event that the physical evidence cannot be effectively appended to the report, it should be completely identified and placed in a safeguarded location with restricted access.

An example of an after-action report can be found in Appendix C.

APPENDIXES

Sample
Security Strike Contingency Plan

(COMPANY)
SECURITY STRIKE CONTINGENCY PLAN

I. INTRODUCTION

Few problems can tax the resources of a facility's security department more than labor disputes that have ended in a strike.

It is the security department's intention to protect company employees and property in the event of a strike and to provide necessary logistical and administrative support to the company's negotiating team.

II. BACKGROUND

A. Description of union

1. Name and address:
International president:
International secretary and treasurer:
International vice presidents:
Regional director:
The above information was taken from:

The objective of the union, according to its constitution, is as follows:

B. Description of union local (number):

1. Name and address:
President:
Vice president:
Secretary/treasurer:
Sergeant-at-arms:
Recording secretary:
Other officers:

C.   Anticipated union reaction

1.   Any strike by the union can be expected to be, at best, a difficult situation.

(Describe anticipated union reaction here)

Depending on the duration of a strike and the particular issues in question, criminal activity, that is, vandalism, harassment, threats, disorderly conduct, and quite possibly assault (inadvertently or by design) should be anticipated.

At best, the company can expect a troublesome time in the event of a strike; at worst, a most trying time.

D.   Description of the company

The company is a Fortune 500 company consisting of 35 divisions in the United States and 10 divisions overseas. The company is essentially an industry-oriented enterprise with some consumer-oriented divisions.

In (state), the company maintains (number) divisions at (number) basic locations, (locations).

Support during labor negotiations and, if necessary, labor disputes can be expected from the corporation and its resources. Since there is no corporate security structure, however, security efforts and resources will have to be directed at the local or division level in accordance with corporate and division strategy.

E.   Description of division

1.   (Location I)

Division headquarters and operations are located in (location) at (address). In addition to the division, the same plot of land is shared by (other divisions and/or companies). The (number) facilities occupy a plot of land bordered on the north by (street), on the south by (street), on the east by (street), and, on the west by (street). The division occupies, roughly, the southernmost third of the area just defined. The division's mailing address is: (address), and its telephone number is: (number).

The division maintains (number) buildings in (location). The first is a (type) building, (color), located on (street). Referred to as "A" building, it houses: (facilities). This building is protected by an (type) alarm system and contains approximately (number) square feet.

The headquarters and administration building contains approximately (number) square feet and is located behind, or west of, "A" building. It houses the executive offices and various administrative functions and is protected by a (type) alarm system. In addition, there is closed circuit TV (CCTV) coverage in this building.

The manufacturing facility, wherein all production operations are performed, is known as "B" building and is protected by a (type) alarm system, CCTV, and other safeguards (describe). The entire division complex is also protected by a uniformed (and armed if appropriate) contract security force supplied by: (name). There is a large parking lot divided into (number) sections, located to the south of all three buildings, and capable of accommodating (number) vehicles.

Authorized entrances/exits and the physical layout of the buildings are illustrated below:

(Place physical layout diagram here)

2. (Location II)

Another division operation is located at: (address) and is housed in a facility owned by (name and address).

This operation occupies the first four floors of an area located in the northern portion of the building. The structure itself is bordered on the north by (street), on the south by (street), on the east by (street), and on the west by (street).

The (second) operation's mailing address and telephone number are:

As previously stated, there is one building housing the division's (second) operation in (location). There is approximately (number) square feet of space used by the operation (in a complex of (number) square feet). The area is protected by a (type) alarm system, CCTV, other safeguards (describe) and a uniformed (and, if applicable, armed) security force. The facility is quite difficult to protect due to its location and design (describe). Authorized entrances/exits and the physical layout of the buildings are illustrated below:

(Place physical layout diagram here)

Other tenants of the building include (if applicable):

(list)

F. Anticipated company security reaction

The security department's basic strategy is to ensure the safety and welfare of all authorized personnel on company property and the protection of company property and assets. The security department intends to comply with all laws and statutes. In addition, it is the security department's intention to assist the division in the furtherance of any legal, division or corporate strategy during a strike.

III. COMPANY SECURITY STRIKE PLAN

A. Chains of command

1. All chains of command will be strictly adhered to unless they are changed by the proper authority in each case, that is, division president or vice president, personnel; director, security; security facility supervisor; guard contractor regional manager.

    2. Chains of command as listed below are attached as appendixes:

        a. Division
        b. Security
        c. Shift
        d. Guard force contractor

B. Government agencies, officials, liaisons

    1. Names, addresses and telephone numbers of appropriate agencies, officials, and liaisons are contained in the attached appendixes

C. Preliminary notifications

    1. The following timetable will be followed regarding preliminary notification of labor negotiations:

    (Date)

    • Advise (police and fire departments) that labor negotiations have commenced
    • Advise sister divisions that labor negotiations have commenced

    (Date)

    • Review special problems with (police and fire departments)

    (Date)

    • In the event of a strike, advise (police and fire departments), sister divisions, utilities, contractors, and vendors

D. Security strike headquarters

The primary security strike headquarters will be located at the security offices in (location), (specific location). This site offers seclusion and added protection due to its location and the resources situated therein, that is, alarm systems, CCTV, and communications.

    An alternate security strike headquarters will be established and occupied, if necessary, at a site to be determined. The alternate security strike headquarters will be equipped with two-way radio and commercial telephone capabilities as well as all pertinent documentation.

E. Initiate and maintain documents

    1. Detailed journal

        a. A detailed daily journal will be maintained in which the following strike-related information only shall be recorded:

            1) Time incident was initiated

2) If it is known, the names of participants initiating the incident. (If it is not known, give as complete a description as possible.)

3) The exact location of the incident. (If the incident takes place in a parking lot or other open area, use accurate measurements and directions from at least two known, fixed landmarks.)

4) A clear, concise narrative description of the actions that caused the incident. (editorializing, opinions, or conclusions will be avoided.)

5) A clear, concise narrative of the actions taken by security personnel to end or control the incident. (Insure that the time the security response is initiated is noted, as well as complete names of all personnel directly involved with the response.)

6) Describe, in detail, actions witnessed by individuals that result in property damage or personal injury, identifying, if possible, the perpetrators of such actions.

7) If outside agency assistance is directed, insure that the time such outside assistance is summoned or requested is noted as well as the time responding personnel actually arrive onsite.

8) When possible, obtain the name and rank of the senior outside agency official present in a command capacity.

9) When the incident is over as determined by (title and name or his designee), ensure that the time is recorded in this journal with a notation that this official (title and name) declared the incident over. This official shall also direct whether the security force personnel are to return to their normal security posture or are to remain at alert posts.

10) The time outside agency response personnel depart the site shall also be recorded.

2. Facility diagrams and maps

a. A supply of expendable facility diagrams and site maps shall be available for personnel at the CCTV (VCR) monitors for use in quickly noting the location of any incidents requiring a security response or any other activity that can be indicative of a developing incident.

b. Personnel at these monitors may use these facility diagrams/site maps to chart the movements of adversary personnel or groups and may indicate, through the insertion of standard symbols (as outlined below), the physical presence of private vehicles, police vehicles and personnel, fire apparatus, and so forth. These diagrams and maps should be numbered in a sequential order.

Initials of CCTV/VCR monitor	Time military clock	Date	Sequential numbering
ABC	0815	01/01/90	1; 2; 3; etc.

Standard diagram symbols

Ⓒ	Company personnel
Ⓢ	Security personnel
Ⓟ	Outside agency response personnel
Ⓧ	Adversary personnel
Ⓕ	Fire personnel
⟨P⟩	Outside agency response vehicle
⟨X⟩	Adversary vehicle
⟨S⟩	Security vehicle
⟨F⟩	Fire apparatus
⟨A⟩	Ambulance or other emergency vehicle
⟨POV⟩	Privately owned vehicle parked on company property

3. Employee lists

    a. It is imperative that security personnel be able to identify quickly and accurately personnel who are authorized for plant access during strike emergency operations. This will require that a list showing nonstriking personnel be provided on a timely basis.

    b. These lists must be accurate and maintained to be up to date by the Personnel Department.

    c. Persons who attempt plant entry whose names do not appear on the list of personnel authorized such access, shall be courteously denied access at the entry point and a security supervisor shall be contacted, provided with the individual's ID data and reason for entry. This supervisor shall contact security management personnel for guidance for each such incident. If security management personnel are unavailable, the security supervisor will contact (member of company management) who will either authorize or deny entry to the individual.

4. Video camera recorders (VCRs)

a. Security personnel assigned the CCTV monitor function shall be completely familiar with VCR operation *prior* to assuming any operational watch.

b. When an incident or potential incident is noted during routine CCTV scanning, which poses a potential for damage to personal property, personnel injury, and so forth, a CCTV camera shall be locked onto the scene, and the VCR shall be activated to record the incident. At the same time, a supervisor shall be notified.

c. When possible, a plant diagram or site map (as applicable) shall be annotated with appropriate diagrams to show the sequence of events. (This written record will supplement the VCR recording and could, in the event of an electronic equipment malfunction, become the only visual record of happenings.)

5. Photographs

a. As a supplement to any hand-executed or VCR record of an incident, whenever possible 35mm still photographs of the incident shall be obtained, paying particular attention to any ringleaders or agitators.

b. If time does not permit the use of 35mm cameras, Polaroid cameras will be used to record incidents or as directed.

6. Union missives

a. Every effort will be made to secure legally any union pamphlets, brochures, flyers, and so forth, either originals or duplicates, and forward them to division management personnel.

F. Initiate electronic surveillance countermeasures
Checks for unauthorized illegal electronic surveillance and appropriate countermeasures will be conducted when a strike appears imminent (or sooner if circumstances dictate). Legal restrictions may preclude certain actions. These should be stated here along with any other laws pertaining to recording and/or overhearing conversations. For example, Connecticut law prohibits "secretive mechanical overhearing and recording of negotiations between employers and employees." At a minimum the following areas will be covered:

1. Company strike headquarters

    2.   Security strike headquarters

    3.   Division negotiating team offices

    4.   Negotiating team telephones

G.   Food service

Arrangements will be made with a suitable vendor to supply meals to security personnel. If this is not possible, security personnel will be directed to supply their own meals.

H.   Establish secure parking areas for nonstrikers at all facilities

    1.   (Location)

        a.   A secure parking area will be maintained at (location). Authorized vehicles will be allowed entry to the parking lot and will be parked in the northernmost section of the salaried and hourly lots in no more than three rows (see diagram). Fourth and fifth rows can be added if necessary. Cars will be parked nose to tail as illustrated. This arrangement will keep vehicles out of range of hand-thrown objects and will allow easy surveillance via CCTV and/or security patrols.

            (Place parking diagram here)

    2.   (Location)

        a.   Secure parking areas will be maintained behind the headquarters and administration building on (street). This area will be monitored via CCTV and/or security patrols.

    3.   Parking alternatives

        a.   An alternative would be to use offsite parking areas and bus nonstrikers to work. This has one major drawback: it would be extremely easy for a striker to identify and locate the offsite parking areas and vandalize nonstrikers' vehicles. A more feasible alternative would be to direct nonstrikers to park independently and bus them from common pickup points throughout the area.

            In any event, nonstriking employees should be directed to carpool whenever possible to limit the number of vehicles requiring protection.

            Nonstrikers' vehicles will be identified by a special parking decal or placard displayed on the outside of the driver's visor while the vehicles are on company property.

I.   Access routes

    1.   (Location)

        a.   All perimeter gates will be closed and securely locked except for the gate on (street) and the gate separating the salaried from the hourly parking lots (Numbers 1 and 1A respectively).

All nonstriking employees, contractors, vendors, shipments, and deliveries will be directed to enter and exit via this route.

2.   (Location)

    a.   Personnel and vehicles authorized access to this facility will park in the designated parking area as indicated on the map.

        Entry will be made off of (street); entrance through the north side of "D" building. Deliveries and shipments will be via Dock (number) (Shipping & Receiving) when necessary.

3.   In the event circumstances dictate, alternate or additional access routes will be established. These routes will be determined at the time they are needed. It is suggested that a secure offsite receiving area be considered to alleviate traffic flow by noncompany vehicles.

J.   Public relations and media inquiries

1.   All members of the security force, without exception, will refer media inquiries to the vice president, personnel, or in his absence, the president (or other designee). If media personnel attempt unauthorized entry onto company property, they will be handled as any other trespasser. The president or the vice president, personnel, or their designees are the only persons authorized to grant access to nonemployees.

K.   Fire protection plan

1.   There are (number) fire extinguishers strategically located at each site. Details, including locations, are maintained at the appropriate security control centers.

2.   Fire extinguishers are inspected and maintained by (company, address, telephone number).

3.   Fires are reported to the appropriate security control center which, in turn, advises maintenance management personnel and dispatches a security officer to the scene with keys. Upon the advice of the senior management person at the scene, the local fire department is notified via a "hot line" or a commercial telephone by the security control center. In the absence of appropriate management personnel, the security shift supervisor has the authority to notify the local fire department. (This particular procedure should be replaced by a site-specific procedure.)

L.   Security personnel deployment

1. Reserve forces
    a. A security strike force comprised of at least (number) additional security officers will supplement the normal contingent at division facilities. This force will be broken down into (number) teams assigned to each facility. Each team member will be unarmed and outfitted in the standard guardforce uniform and equipment. During the hours of darkness, each strike force member may be equipped with a 26-inch baton, handcuffs and flashlight (or other equipment). The strike force will be used primarily for outside patrolling and will augment the existing shift contingent.
    b. Company management personnel
        From the pool of nonstriking employees, a group of selected and screened individuals will be assigned to temporary duty in the security department. Numbers and assignments will be as follows:
        1) Observers: (number) each at (locations)
        2) Photographers: (number) each at (locations)
        3) Stenographers: (number) each at (locations)
        A total of (number) personnel will be required.
    c. Off-duty police officers
        Some jurisdictions, for example, Connecticut, prohibit the use of police officers for strike-related duty. Much consideration must be given to this issue before such a decision is made. At least initially it may be felt that security personnel can handle a strike without involving local police (who would, more than likely, be adverse to getting involved in a strike situation). (Any legal issues regarding this subject would be included here.)
    d. Maintenance personnel
        Depending on the number of nonstriking maintenance personnel, it is suggested that at least two persons at each facility be assigned to temporary duty in the security department and that their time be dedicated solely to maintaining security systems and barriers.
2. Security manning levels
    a. All facilities will operate on a three security shift basis. Each shift will have a basic complement of at least (number) officers. The basic complement may be augmented as necessary. A (number)-man pool will be kept in reserve for deployment as needed. (This is in addition to those previously mentioned.)
3. Additional security force training

a.   A supplemental training program will be given to all security personnel prior to a strike. Highlights of the program include:

   1)   Legal powers and limitations

      a)   Authority and jurisdiction
      b)   Use of force
      c)   Complaint procedures
      d)   Detention and search
      e)   Unfair labor practices

   2)   Officer attitude and conduct

   3)   Crimes usually committed during a strike (appropriate statute references), for example:

      a)   Assault
      b)   Reckless endangerment
      c)   Threatening
      d)   Criminal trespass
      e)   Criminal mischief
      f)   Breach of peace
      g)   Disorderly conduct
      h)   Inciting to riot
      i)   Harassment

   4)   Incidents usually occurring during a strike

      a)   Sabotage
      b)   Vandalism
      c)   Tire slashing
      d)   Tampering with vehicles (ruined auto finishes)
      e)   Bomb threats

The Security Bomb Threat standard operating procedure (SOP) (See subappendix A1) will be implemented and utilized.

Detailed documentation will be maintained for training sessions by the guardforce contractors.

4.   Guardforce contractor's scheduling of hours

The guardforce contractor's facility supervisor will be responsible for scheduling security personnel at least one week in advance of a strike and one week in advance during the strike.

M.   Security department strategy

1.   Security department strategy will be to protect division employees, property, and assets. Any show of force will be avoided unless so directed by (title).

Escalation of tactics or actions by any adversaries will be responded to in an appropriate but *legal* manner.

2. Illegal activity or incidents will be immediately reported to local law enforcement authorities (LLEA). Security personnel will assist LLEA upon *their* request.

3. Security personnel may use only that degree of force necessary to counter the degree of force directed against them.

4. Security personnel will not react or respond to agitation or antagonism directed against them, nor will they engage in any discussion with picket-line participants unless such discussion concerns a medical emergency or an immediate hazard to the general public.

5. Security personnel will be especially alert to attempts to discredit them, the security department, and/or the division. In this regard, a "two-man rule" will be in effect and maintained whenever feasible, that is, security personnel will patrol in pairs or be posted so that each can watch the other.

6. The security department will use all lawful means at its disposal on the direction of the proper authority to ensure the safety of employees and the general public and to protect employees' and company property.

7. Security officers will obey all lawful orders issued by proper authority including orders by LLEA.

8. All division buildings and premises will be physically secured from unauthorized entry to the extent that this is possible. Only authorized entryways may be used by anyone attempting to enter company property.

9. Criminal complaints of offenses against division property will be made by (title). Complaints of offenses against persons will be made only after consultation with (title).

10. Company property will be posted, as necessary, against trespassers.

11. (Person or persons responsible) will brief all company management personnel on security strategy.

N. Equipment and usage
1. Radios
    a. Rental radios will be made available from two separate sources in the event that additional radio communications are required: one source being (name, address, telephone number of company) and the other (name, address, telephone number of company).
    b. A ten-code system will be developed as part of the strike contingency plan. The ten-code system may be used in the event of a strike and the use of such a system will be strictly adhered to. No names and/or sensitive information will be given during radio transmissions. Telephones normally will be used whenever possible.

2.   CCTV

a.   A brief description of each camera location and its capabilities will be posted in each control center to monitor any alarms in the scanning vicinity of that camera. At the direction of (title), videotape recordings will be made. (ID data will be painted in the viewing area of each camera.)

3.   Portable alarms

a.   At least two microwave motion detectors will be set up on tripods. These units will be adapted so that they may be tied into the existing alarm system wherever this is deemed necessary.

4.   Extra lighting

a.   At least two sets of extra lights will be made available to the security department from the maintenance department. The basic fixture will be two spotlights mounted on a tripod or other device along with a 100-foot extension cord so that they may be used wherever necessary.

b.   Additional lighting should be permanently installed in the parking lot near the (street) entrance in the (location) facility.

c.   Any lights, permanent or temporary, should be protected by a plexiglass-type material to prevent breakage from rocks or other missiles.

5.   Magnets and brooms

a.   These items will be located in each security control center. This equipment will be used to clear paved areas at the entrances to both facilities of foreign materials that may have been placed there to cause damage to vehicles coming onto company property. Objects of concern are nails, glass, or other sharp objects that might cause damage to vehicles. If at all possible, the use of water hoses should be considered.

6.   Scott air pack

a.   One Scott air pack should be immediately available to security at each facility. It would be used by security in the event of fire, heavy smoke, or chemical gases. Necessary training will be provided. Each maintenance department will also have a Scott air pack that can be used by security.

7.   Gas masks

a.   Two military-type gas masks should be immediately available to security at each facility to be used as necessary.

8. Photographic equipment
   a. The following is a list of photo equipment that should be available to the security department.
      1) 35mm camera(s) with telephoto lens
      2) Fixed VCR recording unit(s)
      3) Portable VCR unit(s)
      4) Polaroid camera(s)
   b. Supervisory personnel will be trained in the use of the above equipment and will be briefed on incidents and/or situations that should be photographed. Additional equipment will be procured if necessary.

9. Generators
   a. Emergency generators will be kept readily available to security personnel. These generators will be used to power the alarm system, radio system, emergency lighting, and so forth, in case of power failure.

10. Weapons
    a. Firearms (if applicable and/or appropriate)
       1) Firearms will be issued only to those persons in the security department who normally carry them. The normal firearms policy will be in effect. Additional weapons issued to security personnel will be at the direction of the (title) and only to those persons who have been properly trained and certified and licensed by the state. Firearms are for defensive purposes only, that is, to protect a person in imminent danger of death or grievous bodily harm.
    b. Mace
       1) The carrying and/or use of mace will be at the discretion of the (title).
          (Discuss applicable state law here)
    c. Batons
          (Discuss applicable law here)
    d. All security personnel will be properly trained in the use and application of the above weapons as necessary.

11. Portable guardhouses
    a. Identify availability of portable guardhouses, if any.

12. Equipment checks will be made daily to ensure operability.

O. Access controls
   1. To facilities
      a. All nonstriking employees and others with authorized access during a strike will be issued a different and dis-

tinctive employee ID badge or tamperproof sticker for identification purposes. No one will be allowed in any division facilities without such a badge or sticker. Badges will bear the photograph of the holder and must be worn at all times while on company property.

 b. The escort requirement for controlled areas at facilities will be strictly enforced. In addition, certain other areas will be designated by security, maintenance, and manufacturing management as "sensitive areas." A "two-man rule" will be strictly enforced in all sensitive areas.

 2. To premises

  a. Anyone desiring entry onto division property will be permitted to do so with the approval of a member of (company) management.

P. Reporting requirements

 1. Daily reports

  a. All paperwork will be collected by the first shift supervisor every morning no later than (time). The first shift supervisor will separate and coordinate all paperwork into proper sections. The facility supervisor will pick up this paperwork each morning at (time). The facility supervisor will be responsible for coordinating, reviewing, and submitting all the proper paperwork to the (title). Any and all paperwork requiring involvement of persons other than security personnel will be done at the discretion of the (title).

  b. All paperwork is to be submitted by (time) daily.

 2. Weekly reports

  a. It will be the responsibility of the facility supervisor to compile a weekly incident report that will be submitted at (time) every Friday.

Q. Special orders

 1. Special orders will be found in the corresponding attached appendix.

R. Miscellaneous items

 1. Any items not previously covered will be found in the corresponding attached appendix.

Note: Appendices containing the following information are generally found at the end of a strike contingency plan:

1. Listing of union district leadership including name, title, date of birth, address, telephone number, automobile description, and registration information.

2. Listing of local union leadership including name, title, date of birth, address, telephone number, automobile description, and registration information.
3. Listing of local union stewards including name, address, company ID number, department number, and supervisor.
4. Listing of corporate leaders including title, corporate headquarters address, and telephone number.
5. Listing of division leadership including name and title.
6. Listing of division chain of command (organizational chart).
7. Listing of security chain of command.
8. Listing of contract security chain of command.
9. Listing of the operating shift chain of command.
10. Listing of state and local agencies and liaisons including title, name, address, and office telephone number. (The list should include police, fire, state labor commissioner, and local government representatives.)
11. Listing of miscellaneous contacts with telephone numbers including emergency and routine police, fire, and ambulance service; local radio, TV, and newspapers; electric, gas, and water company emergency numbers; company emergency numbers; company medical department personnel; and contract security corporate information.
12. Listing of company key personnel including name, title, home address, and telephone number.
13. Listing of the location(s) of firefighting equipment (maintained at security control).
14. Listing of management personnel assigned to various security locations (to be completed as necessary).
    a.   (Location)
    b.   Console
    c.   CCTV
    d.   Video team
    e.   Video team
15. Listing of maintenance personnel assigned to security (to be completed as necessary).
16. Listing of special orders.

Also found at the end of the strike contingency plan are sections on the bomb threat SOP, miscellaneous items, and employee briefing.

SUBAPPENDIX A1
THE BOMB THREAT SOP (EXAMPLE)

I.   *Response by recipients of bomb threats*

    A.   *General*

        If, at any time, someone receives a bomb threat, he or she will immediately advise the appropriate security control center. Such threats can be made via a variety of means, for example, by telephone or mail; however, most threats are received by telephone.

    B.   *Bomb threat checklist*

        Keep the caller on the phone as long as possible. Questions to ask:

        1.   When is bomb going to explode?

        2.   Where is it right now?

        3.   What does it look like?

        4.   What kind of bomb is it?

        5.   What will cause it to explode?

        6.   Did you place the bomb?

        7.   Why?

        8.   What is your address?

        9.   What is your name?

Ask the caller to repeat the message. Record every word spoken. If the caller does not indicate the location of the bomb or the time of possible detonation, ask for this information.

Inform the caller that the building is occupied and the detonation of a bomb could result in death or serious injury to many innocent people.

Pay particular attention to peculiar background noises such as motors running, background music, and any other noise that may give a clue about the location of the caller.

Listen closely to the voice (male, female), voice quality (calm, excited), accents, and speach impediments. Immediately after the caller hangs up, report the threat to security. Since law enforcement personnel will want to talk first-hand with the person who received the call, remain available.

Report the following immediately to security:

Exact wording of the threat: _____

_____

Sex of caller: _____ Race: _____

Age: _____ Length of call: _____

Number at which call was received: _____

Time: _____ Date: _____

Caller's voice:

_____ Calm	_____ Nasal
_____ Angry	_____ Stutter
_____ Excited	_____ Lisp
_____ Slow	_____ Raspy
_____ Rapid	_____ Deep
_____ Soft	_____ Rugged
_____ Loud	_____ Clearing throat
_____ Laughter	_____ Deep breathing
_____ Crying	_____ Cracking voice
_____ Normal	_____ Disguised
_____ Distinct	_____ Accent
_____ Slurred	_____ Familiar

If voice is familiar, who did it sound like? _____

_____

Background sounds:

_____ Street noises	_____ Factory machinery
_____ Crockery	_____ Animal noises
_____ Voices	_____ Clear
_____ Static	_____ PA system
_____ Music	_____ Local
_____ Long distance	_____ House noises
_____ Motor	_____ Booth
_____ Office machinery	_____ Other (Explain) _____

_____

_____

Threat language:

_____ Well spoken	_____ Incoherent
_____ Foul	_____ Taped
_____ Irrational	_____ Message read by threat maker

REPORT CALL IMMEDIATELY TO SECURITY!

Date: _____

Name: _____

Position: _____

Phone: _____

II. *Security response to bomb threats*

  A. *General*

  Upon notification that a bomb threat has been received, the on-duty security supervisor will:

  1. Suspend all two-way radio communications and advise *all* security personnel via an alternate means.

  2. Initiate and maintain a comprehensive chronological incident report.

  3. Immediately contact the guardforce facility supervisor and the local police department. (If the guardforce supervisor cannot be contacted, attempt to contact the [title]. The guardforce facility supervisor will immediately contact the [title] and then respond to the scene.)

  4. Establish a command post at the *security control center* of the affected facility or facilities. Advise all security personnel of this location, and answer all incoming telephone calls. Media inquiries should be referred to the (title) during normal business hours.

  5. Advise the senior person at the affected facility and request that he or she organize a search of the premises in conjunction with security personnel. Maintenance personnel as well as supervisory personnel should be used as their knowledge of the facility and areas within is extensive. *All searchers must, however, be volunteers.*

  6. Assemble all searchers into teams at the *command post* and search the control center and adjacent areas thoroughly. If anything suspicious is discovered, it must not be touched, and the information should be relayed to law enforcement authorities. If a suspicious item *is* discovered in or near the security control center, an alternate command post should be set up (after it has been searched) at another location, which has a telephone. All security personnel should be advised of the new location and phone number.

  7. Stand by to

    a. Direct a search of the entire premises

    b. Effect an orderly evacuation (through security systems if circumstances permit) if this is ordered by law enforcement authorities at the scene or by the (title)

III. *Management response to bomb threats*

  A. *General*

  Every bomb threat must be assessed and an appropriate course of action determined. It is therefore crucial that the information in part I be obtained if at all possible. Among the factors for assessing the credibility of a bomb threat are:

1.   The content of the warning, that is, the extent and accuracy of the information provided by the caller especially the time the bomb is to explode and its location

2.   Recent developments concerning the company that could precipitate a bomb being placed or a threat of same, for example, labor difficulties and antiwar protests

3.   The opportunity a bomber might have had to place an explosive device

One of the most difficult processes in dealing with bomb threats is assessing their credibility and making the decision about whether to evacuate a facility. In any event, personnel safety is the overriding consideration in any decision.

B.   *Evacuation*
The decision to evacuate a facility can only be made by law enforcement authorities on the scene or by the management personnel in the order listed below.

(list)

If evacuation is ordered by one of the individuals listed above, evacuees are to assemble by department in areas designated by law enforcement authorities or by the senior management person on the scene.

C.   *Reentry*
If the threat proves to be a hoax, reoccupation of the facilities can only be ordered, after receipt of an all-clear from the law enforcement authorities at the scene, by the same person who ordered the evacuation. Under no circumstances will employees be allowed to leave early or will arriving shifts be canceled without the approval of the (title) or, in his or her absence, the person ordering the evacuation.

D.   *Discovery of explosive devices*
In the event an explosive device is found, all further directions will come from law enforcement authorities until an all-clear is given by them.

E.   *Detonation of an explosive device*
If an explosion occurs, it will be responded to in a manner appropriate to the circumstances.

SUBAPPENDIX A2
MISCELLANEOUS ITEMS

I.   If necessary, conduct briefings for appropriate personnel regarding:

    A.   Vehicle escorts

    B.   Housechecks

    C.   Nonstriker's conduct (for example, crossing picket lines)

    D.   Offsite receiving location

II. Offsite receiving facilities
    The following warehouse companies have been selected to receive materials during a strike situation:

    A.   Primary:

        1.   Name:

        2.   Location:

        3.   Telephone:

        4.   Point of contact:

    B.   Alternate:

        1.   Name:

        2.   Location:

        3.   Telephone:

        4.   Point of contact:

The primary or alternate company will receive material from all trucking except (list). All material received will be palletized and picked up by company trucks as soon as possible. The receiving company will sign for all material they receive, and this will be verified upon pickup. Other items will be picked up by the company's truck.
Both locations can only handle (list).

SUBAPPENDIX A3
EMPLOYEE BRIEFING

I.   *Vehicle identification*

    A.   Scrape off old stickers and/or anything associated with the company.

    B.   A vehicle identification card will be used. Enter ID number in appropriate block.

        1.   Do not locate card on outside of vehicle.

        2.   Place card on dashboard and display it when you are on company property. Remove and hide it at all other times.

II. *Crossing a picket line with a vehicle*

    A.   Police and security will be on duty.

    B.   Lock all doors.

    C.   Roll up all windows.

        1.   Do not open windows or door for anyone unless you are so directed by a police officer.

    D.   Do not strike picketers.

    E.   Watch the police officer. Briefings were held so the police are aware of the situation.

    F.   Car pool whenever possible. Keep vehicles to minimum. Do not exit vehicle under any circumstances until it is parked.

    G.   Avoid entering the plant from (state any restrictions).

        1.   Entrances/exits are at Gate 1 (street) and at the gate on (street).

III. *Entrances/exits and parking*

    A.   Entrances/exits

        1.   (Street) entrances are for vehicles and personnel.

            a.   Alternate entrances/exits will be used as necessary. You will be advised.

            b.   Personnel will enter/exit the facility through the barrier line.

    B.   Parking

        1.   Locations—explanation

        2.   Security officers will be in the parking area to direct parking for the first few days.

IV. *Employee identification*

    A.   ID badges are to be worn at all times while you are on company property. This means in all buildings. There are no exceptions.

B. Visitor badges will be issued by the security officer on duty in the parking lot.

V. *Conduct and attitudes during a strike*

    A. If possible, do not *walk* through the picket lines.

    B. Do not converse with picket line participants.

    C. Do not allow yourself to be agitated.

    D. No weapons are to be carried.

    E. Travel in pairs whenever possible.

    F. Try not to leave premises for lunch. The canteen will provide meals.

    G. Be alert to unauthorized persons (without ID badges) on premises. Call security.

    H. Unless it is an emergency, keep requests of security to a minimum.

    I. Use routine security telephone numbers except for emergencies.

        1. (Location) routine: extensions (numbers)

        2. (Location) emergency: extensions (numbers)

    J. If you contact security after hours, you will be asked to identify yourself by name, ID number, and telephone number. Hang up and security will immediately return your call.

    K. If anything happens to you that could be strike-related, for example, harassing phone calls, contact your local police department. Advise security as soon as possible after you have notified the police.

    L. Be alert to safety, especially if you are assigned to a machine or operation. Make sure you obtain the necessary training and safety orientation from your supervisor. Some of you will be operating machines that you have not operated for a long time or at all.

B

Sample Emergency Plan

(COMPANY)
EMERGENCY PLAN (EXAMPLE)
HURRICANE (NAME AND DATE)

Prepared by:
Distribution:

Contents

I. *Company policy*
    It is (company) policy to prepare for the hurricane's landfall and thus provide for the safety and well being of all employees and visitors as well as minimize and control property damage to facilitate a speedy recovery after the hurricane has passed.

II. *Purpose of this plan*
    The purpose of this plan is to incorporate all employee safety, damage control, and recovery considerations into one document that will serve to guide the total effort, to delineate authority, and to delegate responsibilities in furtherance of the policy stated above.

III. *Authority for this plan*
    Authority for this plan is derived from the president and Crisis Management Team (CMT). Specific authority to implement and to supervise jointly the implementation of this plan is delegated by the president and the CMT to the (title[s]).

IV. *Basic information regarding hurricanes*
    The following basic facts about hurricanes (not in any particular order of priority) may provide some understanding of the phenomenon and better prepare for its effect:

    A. Winds move in a counterclockwise direction in the northern hemisphere.
    B. Winds of at least 74 MPH are necessary for a storm to be classified as a hurricane.
    C. Two "fuels" must be present for a hurricane to form and be sustained: moist air and heat.
    D. The eye of a hurricane may be 10 to 20 miles across.
    E. The heaviest rains come from clouds surrounding the eye of the storm.
    F. The eye itself is clear.
    G. The normal sequence of activity is: wind and rain at the onset of the storm, a period of calm and clear sky, then another period of rain and wind, this time in the opposite direction. (This sequence assumes the observer is in the eye's path.)
    H. Generally, hurricanes in the northern hemisphere move westward with the trade winds and then turn northward.
    I. Hurricanes "die" when the "fuel" supply is cut off (that is, over land or over colder ocean areas).
    J. In a 24 hour period, 6–10 inches or more of rain often falls.
    K. The greatest damage on land is from flooding; strong winds also result in damage.

    Once a hurricane watch has been announced, approximately 36 hours will elapse before a warning is issued. After a warning is issued, landfall will occur sometime in the next 24 hours.

V.   *Assessment of company's vulnerability*
If the hurricane strikes (location) with anything close to full force, the company can reasonably expect moderate to severe damage to its facilities. If the storm approaches from the south, the ridge to the south, at the edge of company property *may* mitigate its effects to an unknown extent. The hurricane's likely approach will be from the (direction).

The company's status may make the storm's effects more profound. Because of the nature of its product and of the raw materials on hand, security and safeguards efforts cannot be abandoned or compromised.

Areas of specific concern include, but are not necessarily limited to:

(list)

Several areas have been determined to be personnel safe due to their construction and/or location. They are:

(list)

Again, this list is not all inclusive.

In addition, secondary effects on the facilities would more than likely include loss of utilities (gas, water, and electricity), of phone service, and possibly of two-way radio service to locations offsite.

There are undoubtedly other specific areas that could be of concern.

VI. *Communication and coordination with outside agencies*
Once a landfall is expected (that is, a hurricane warning is issued), communications and coordination with the state police, the fire company, and as far as possible state civil-preparedness authorities will follow. In addition, a weather hotline will have been established for the storm. The telephone number is (number).

VII. *Internal communications and coordination*
Upon implementation of this plan, communications and coordination will follow with security, emergency director(s), safety plant services, maintenance, emergency services, operations, and personnel.
Appropriate communications with employees should be initiated and maintained as necessary by personnel.

In addition, volunteers from the employee population should be solicited to augment onsite emergency management and response and security personnel to allow the latter to function as intended. Volunteers could be used to record preevent, event and postevent activities; assist with recovery and clean-up operations; and relieve personnel (as appropriate) if the duration of the storm and its aftermath are protracted.

VIII. *Responsibilities*
The president is responsible for convening the CMT to address preparations for the storm.

The CMT is responsible for approving a plan for dealing with the emergency, assigning authority and responsibility for implementation of the approved plan, and monitoring the process of preparation and recovery activities.

The (title) is responsible for implementation of the approved plan, compliance with its requirements, and designation of personnel to support the plan.

Designated security, safety, emergency services, plant services, maintenance, operations, and personnel employees are responsible for assisting with the implementation of the approved plan.

IX.   *Emergency management organization*
(Place organization chart here.)

X.   *Warning systems, early release of employees, and shift cancellations*
The National Weather Service (NWS) will provide advisories and warnings. All actions will be predicated on this agency's forecasts.

If landfall is expected during operating hours, the CMT will authorize early release of employees. Personnel will arrange for early release and ensure that any visitors onsite have been advised.

If landfall is expected during nonoperating hours, the CMT will decide whether to cancel subsequent shifts. In the event that shifts are canceled, personnel will ensure that employees are advised via local stations. Resident nonemployees will also be kept informed by personnel.

XI.   *Emergency control center (ECC)*
The (location) will serve as the ECC. It will be equipped with private, commercial, and radio telephone service; direct phone service (hot lines) to state police; two-way radio communications onsite and offsite. In addition, the ECC contains the in-plant public address (PA) system. It is a secure location and is equipped to operate on emergency power.

XII.   *Communications capabilities*
In addition to those communications capabilities noted in XI above, other capabilities exist:

A.   A portable PA system.

B.   A bullhorn.

C.   An amateur radio (HAM) network, operated by FCC-licensed employees, is available for use during this contingency. Stations will be located at:
(list)

A battery-powered AM-FM radio will be located within the facility in a "safe" area and will be monitored for pertinent information.

XIII.   *Emergency shutdown procedures*
Section A in the appendix to this plan contains emergency shutdown procedures.

XIV.   *Contingency equipment and supplies*
The following contingency equipment and supplies should be available onsite in sufficient quantities:

A.   Rope

B.   Blankets

C.   Cots

D.   Plastic sheeting

E.   Plywood

F.   Tarps

G.   "Hot stick"

H.   Goggles

I.   Hard hats/helmets

J.   Fire extinguishers

K.   Tools

L.   Bolt cutters

M.   Coveralls

N.   Portable generators

O.   Security equipment and supplies

P.   Firefighting equipment and supplies

Q.   Medical equipment and supplies

R.   Batteries

S.   Emergency lights

T.   Flashlights

U.   Chainsaw

Fixed generators have been "topped off" and extra gasoline will be procured and stored in accordance with safety requirements. In addition, all company vehicles will be "topped off" and their fuel used if and when necessary.

A supply of warning flares will be procured and stored in accordance with safety requirements.

Extra propane for forklifts will be procured and stored in accordance with safety requirements.

XV.   *Staffing*
At a minimum, the facility will be staffed by the following personnel:
(list)
This is a total of (number) people.

XVI.   *Food/water*
The company food vendor will be asked to provide enough food, juices, and soda to sustain (number) people for (number) days. Their

freezers must be capable of maintaining a freezing level for approximately 24 hours in the event of a loss of electrical power.

Plant services will procure six-gallon jugs of drinking water and store them in one of the identified personnel-safe areas.

Maintenance will set up a well (or another source if possible) for pumping water for washing and sanitary purposes.

XVII. *Sanitation requirements*

The company food vendor will be asked to provide a sufficient quantity of paper plates, plastic utensils, and garbage bags.

A supply of paper towels and soap will be available for use by onsite personnel.

Maintenance will be asked to supply water for flushing to at least one toilet if possible. Alternatively buckets of water from an onsite well will be used for this purpose.

If it is feasible and possible, an existing shower facility will be put into service.

XVIII. *Preparations*

All radio batteries will be brought up to a full charge (and then removed as soon as power to the charging unit is lost).

Storm drains and culverts will be checked and, if necessary, cleared.

Signboard letters, trash containers, and exterior ashtrays will be removed.

Yard:

A.   All loose objects will be picked up or secured.

B.   Barrels will be secured as much as possible.

C.   Emergency generator's fuel supplies will be checked and topped off if necessary.

D.   Loose objects will be removed from roofs.

E.   Construction/repair projects:

    1.   All loose siding/steel will be moved into corners.

    2.   Purlings will be battened down.

    3.   Siding will be supported where possible.

F.   As much material as possible will be moved to shelter.

G.   Other areas will be checked and emergency measures taken as necessary.

H.   Glass windows will be taped.

I.   Trailers will be lashed down whenever possible.

J.   Dumpster covers will be closed and secured; if necessary, dumpsters will be tied down.

K.   Inside water flows (for example, sinks) will be checked and if necessary shut off.

L. Measures will be taken to protect/preserve computer hardware/software.

M. As much patching material as possible will be stored inside "safe" areas.

N. *Soft* areas will be reinforced.

O. Vehicles remaining onsite will be parked bumper to bumper in the middle of the main parking lot with at least a five-foot separation between rows. Company vehicles will be parked on the outside edge of this parking configuration.

P. Portable generators will be readied for use and deployed.

Q. Power to nonessential areas will be shut off.

R. Processing gas supplies will be shut off.

S. Exhaust systems will be shut down.

T. Power-down procedures will be put into effect as necessary.

U. Commercial electricity and gas will be shut off as necessary.

XIX. *Security operations*

A. The normal security condition will be increased as appropriate, consistent with the crisis management plan.

B. (Regulatory agencies) will be advised of anticipated compensatory measures.

C. If necessary, certain guard posts will be abandoned and appropriate compensatory measures instituted.

D. If necessary, shuttle service will be provided for personnel without vehicles or for those wishing to leave their vehicles at home.

E. In the event of an employee release, outgoing traffic will be expedited at (location) and police authorities advised.

F. Temporary guard posts will be established as necessary. All such measures will be fully documented.

G. Additional equipment will be issued as necessary.

H. Additional security personnel will be scheduled as appropriate.

I. Additional interior patrols will be initiated and maintained.

J. A set of codes will be communicated in advance and used as necessary to advise those appropriate agencies of company status and security posture.

XX. *Other considerations*
Consideration should be given to:

A. Media inquiries

B. An evacuation plan

XXI. *Recovery*

After the storm has passed, a damage assessment will be made and a specific checklist formulated to address recovery operations. That checklist will be attached to this plan as an appendix and will include, but not necessarily be limited to, recall of employees, rotation of personnel, use of personnel, emergency financial considerations, emergency repair and restoration of facilities and equipment, and utilities repair and restoration.

XXII. *References*

(list)

XXIII. *Appendix*

A. Appendixes containing the following information are also found at the end of an emergency plan.

1. The listing of emergency shutdown procedures

2. The recovery plan (see Chapter 11 for description)

3. The decision/action matrix

B. *Decisions/actions (upon announcement of hurricane watch)*

1. First priority

a. Communication to employees

b. Charge batteries fully

c. Continue to monitor NWS

2. Second priority

a. Schedule security and emergency response personnel

b. Alert security and emergency response personnel

c. Procure six-gallon water jugs

d. Top off company vehicles with gasoline

e. Place hold on stores items

3. Third priority

a. Procure extra propane for forklifts

b. Make preparations

c. Develop radio codes

4. Fourth priority

a. Set up well to pump water (maintenance to do this)

C. *Decisions/actions (hurricane warning issued)*

1. First priority

a. Prepare and plan photodocument effort

b. Arrange for food, paper plates, plastic utensils, and garbage bags

   c. Procure and store paper towels and soap in area designated as "safe"

   d. Communicate and coordinate with CMT, security, safety, operations (maintenance, plant services, and production), emergency director(s), personnel, and government representatives as appropriate

   e. Continue to monitor NWS

  2. Second priority

   a. Procure and store extra gasoline

   b. Secure and store emergency equipment inside a "safe" area

   c. Set up a HAM network (state police, fire department, and other locations)

   d. Notify regulatory agencies (as appropriate) regarding preparations, planning, and communication

  3. Third priority

   a. Direct food service vendor to procure food

   b. Set up supply of "flush" water (or provide for buckets and water source)

   c. Communicate and coordinate with:

        (list)

  4. Fourth priority

   a. Continue preparations as above

   b. Release employees/cancel shifts

 D. *Decisions/actions (landfall)*

  1. First priority

   a. Continue to monitor NWS

  2. Second priority

   a. Go to contingency mode of operations

   b. Assign personnel onsite to "safe" areas

   c. Assign security personnel as necessary

 E. *Decisions/actions (recovery)*

  1. Priorities

   a. Develop the recovery plan

   b. Implement the recovery plan

   c. Photodocument the facility and the aftereffects of the storm

XXIV. *Documentation*

A Special Events Log will be initiated and maintained as directed by (title).

C

Sample Afteraction Report

HURRICANE (NAME AND DATE)

Distribution:

Contents

Background

On (date), Hurricane (name) made landfall in the vicinity of (location). Its effects were felt all along the (state) shoreline and inland into (state). (State) and (state) were also affected by the hurricane.

The (company) facilities at (location[s]) were subjected to the storm starting at approximately (time) on (date). At that time, increasing winds and some rainfall was observed. These effects increased in intensity, particularly the winds, until the hurricane had passed at approximately (time) on (date).

The following is a chronological account of the measures, actions, reports, and so forth, (company) personnel took prior to, during, and after the storm. It represents the best effort to reconstruct the events as they occurred and to record the times that they happened. Times are as accurate as possible given some disparity in the various sources of information used in compiling this report. Information herein was extracted from several sources including (company security) duty logs, special events journal, National Hurricane Center (NHC) advisories, National Weather Service (NWS) reports, handwritten notes, radio and TV reports, telephonic and radio messages, and personal recollections.

Measures Taken Prior to Hurricane (name)

(Date—Day 1)

As soon as it became apparent that the hurricane posed a threat to (location) in general and (company facilities) in particular, an intensive and extensive planning effort commenced. It was decided to base actions/decisions on NWS/NHC information. Constant monitoring of NWS broadcasts from (location) and calls to the NHC Hotline were initiated.

1045—NWS update received.

1251—NWS update received.

1440—NWS update received.

1600—A meeting was held in/at (location to review preparations for the possible impact of the hurricane. In attendance were:
(list)

(Name) presented a list of several items to be addressed in preparation for the hurricane. (Name) presented a draft announcement for the bulletin boards to inform the employees of activities related to the storm. (Name) presented a comprehensive list of items being reviewed, both security and nonsecurity. Some items were already underway (for example, clean-up of loose items outdoors, identification of required personnel, and topping off of emergency generator fuel tanks).

Among the items discussed were potential for product damage and possible protective measures, safety concerns (for example, flying objects, gas line breaks, and window breaks), compensatory measures in the event of systems failures, avenues of communication, procedures if and when phone lines went out, food and water for emergency and security personnel, notification to regulatory agencies, employee notification and evacuation, necessary emergency services personnel (fire brigade, EMTs, nurses, and safety), shutdown of critical operations in anticipation of power failures, required maintenance and security personnel, definition of lines of authority, and maintenance of records associated with the preparation and actual event. (Name) will coordinate with (name) in the preparation efforts. The group decided to reconvene on (date) to decide on actions to be taken that day, considering the weather predictions available at that time.

> 1700—A set of "status codes" was developed to ensure accurate reporting of security status during the storm if all normal communications were disrupted and plant status had to be broadcast. An amateur radio network, that is, a HAM network, was assembled to deal with this exigency if it became necessary.

(Date—Day 2)

A teletype link between (company) and the NHC in Coral Gables, Florida was established and written advisories were obtained on a continuing basis. In addition, monitoring of NWS broadcasts continued.

> 0600—NHC Advisory 37 was received. (Advisories are attached in Appendix I).
>
> 0800—A meeting was held to review the latest weather forecast relative to hurricane (name) and actions to be taken based on that information. In attendance were:
>
> (list)

Latest forecasts say the storm is headed NW toward (location) and that the effect on this area will most likely be limited to heavy rains and strong winds on (date). (Name) presented a typed list of decisions/actions in a phased order (hurricane watch, warning, landfall, and recovery) that will be followed by a typed plan (Appendix II). He reviewed portions of that plan that dealt with the first-phase actions (Phase A actions). The status of some of the preliminary actions undertaken on (date)—(yard cleanup, supply procurement, and so forth) was discussed. It was decided to proceed with the Phase A items that were not already underway, to continue to monitor the storm's progress, and to reconvene at 1300 this date to review the status of actions underway and decide on any additional actions to be taken at that time.

> 0830—NWS update received.
> 0930—NWS update received.
> 1030—NWS update received.

1200—Emergency services and maintenance staffing was suggested by (name) based on different skills, abilities, and cross-training to provide an ideal mix of talent available from the limited number of personnel remaining onsite.

—Empty Scott cylinders were in the process of being refilled.

—A chain saw was purchased by security for use by the fire brigade.

—Emergency services equipment was being checked.

—Fire brigade two-way radios were being checked.

—Temporary cabs were being installed on open company vehicles to protect personnel and communications equipment in case their use during the storm became necessary.

—A contingency schedule for security personnel was developed, and all affected personnel were alerted. Volunteers were used whenever possible.

—Full, six-gallon jugs of drinking water were located and their locations identified.

—All company vehicles were to be topped off and stored in (location) at the close of the work day.

—Extra propane for forklifts was located and its location identified.

—Preparations previously identified were continuing.

—NHC Advisory 38 was received.

1300—A meeting was held in/at (location) to review the contingency plan developed by (name), and the latest weather bureau advisory (that had been received at 1200). The storm has assumed a NNW direction with an increased, but still low, probability of landfall in this general area at about (day/time). In attendance were the same people as were at the 0800 meeting plus:

(list)

It was decided to proceed with implementation of the plan, to post an update on the storm status after receiving the 1500 advisory, to establish guidelines for off-shift security supervision to initiate management notification, for (name) to calculate the ability of (sensitive locations/equipment) to withstand wind loading, and to meet again at 0800 (day) morning, (date).

1445—Word was received that a hurricane watch and gale warnings were issued by the NWS.

1700—Preparations in accordance with the Emergency Plan for hurricane (name) continued.

—NHC Advisory 39 (time of issue, 1500) was received. It confirmed that a hurricane watch and gale warnings were in effect.

—(Names) reviewed this latest advisory and decided to wait for the next update, which was due at 1800, as well as proceeding to alert those employees who had volunteered to staff the site during a storm. (Name), in a later contact, agreed with that action plan.

2145—The situation was monitored by management at home. (Name) checked periodically with the facility on the progress of preparations and for the next NHC Advisory.

2149—NHC Advisory (no number) was received. It posed a hurricane warning for the area inlcuding (location). This information was relayed to management personnel.

—Efforts continued to determine a precise time that the hurricane would make landfall. These efforts were hampered by the lack of sufficient information from the NHC as well as the various, and often diverse, TV and radio news reports.

(Date—Day 3)

0550—NHC Advisory 41 was received. (If there was a number 40, it was never received despite constant monitoring.) It indicated that the center of the storm would pass, ". . . over (location) later today."

0600—(Estimated)—(names) conferred regarding a telephone call from (name) urging that the first shift be canceled. An attempt was made to call (name). He had, however, already left his home for the plant. It was decided that, due to the NHC estimate (previous entry), a decision effecting plant closing could be deferred until a 0730 meeting scheduled for management personnel.

0700—A complete system phone check was made. Everything was O.K.

0715—NHC Advisory 42 was received. It advised that (hurricane name) ". . . is expected to further increase forward (north) speed as it moves near the (location) and the (location) coast by midday and to near (location) by *midafternoon* [Emphasis added]."

0730—A meeting was held to review the situation. In attendance were:
(list)
Based on the latest forecasts, it was estimated that the hurricane would hit the state coastline around the (location) area between 1100 and 1500. The decision was made, therefore, to announce that the plant would close at 0815 and that second shift would be canceled.

0800—An emergency HAM radio station was set up in (location) and staffed by (names). This station had five separate radio frequencies through three repeater systems and was capable of outside communication in the event of a total communications failure resulting from the storm.

0810—Regulatory agencies were contacted and advised of the company's preparations and status codes.

0815—(Estimated)—Corporate offices were advised of the company's status by (name).

Actions Taken during the Storm

(Date)

0818—The facility was shut down and second shift was canceled. Volunteers were solicited to assist during the storm. The following announcement was made on the P.A. system.

"The plant will be shut down at this time. Second shift is canceled. Please feel free to leave at any time. Also, please be careful in leaving the parking lot. If anyone would like to volunteer to remain on-site to assist, please contact the security office in (location). We need (number) additional volunteers."

—The following personnel remained onsite, in addition to security guards:

	Name	Dept	Status
1.			Volunteer
2.			Volunteer
3.			Volunteer (out 1630)
4.			Volunteer (out 1615)
5.			Volunteer
6.			Volunteer
7.			MRT
8.			Fire brigade coordinator
9.			Fire brigade/EMT
10.			Fire brigade/MRT
11.			Fire brigade/EMT
12.			Fire brigade
13.			Fire brigade
14.			Fire brigade/MRT
15.			Fire brigade/MRT
16.			Facilities maintenance
17.			Facilities maintenance
18.			Security/HAM operator
19.			Volunteer/HAM operator
20.			Equipment maintenance
21.			Facilities maintenance
22.			Equipment maintenance
23.			Equipment maintenance
24.			Equipment maintenance
25.			Security
26.			Security
27.			Security

28.   Security

29.   Security

30.   Security site administrator

31.   Facilities maintenance/HAM
                                       operator

32.   Offsite volunteer/HAM operator

—The fire/rescue brigade was assembled, briefed by (name), and split into three groups. One group was assigned to the fire station, the second group was to patrol the interior of the plant at specific intervals, and the third group was stationed at the safety office in (location). All groups were equipped with two-way radios and all personnel were issued pocket pagers.

—Security personnel operated the traffic lights at (locations) to facilitate employees' departure.

0830—(Name, title, other location) called and advised that that location's contingency plan was in effect. (Contingency measures had been coordinated earlier.)

0835—Lieutenant (name) of the state police (location), approved placement of mobil HAM operator at that location for emergency communications should they become necessary. Use of the HAM network was offered to Lieutenant (name) as a public relations gesture.

0845—After repeated, unsuccessful attempts to contact (regulatory agency) in (location) by commercial telephone, (name) contacted (name and agency) and asked to relay a clarification of status codes to (name, location) and said he would also do so. He was further advised that a HAM radio network had been set up as a contingency measure. (Name) supplied a frequency of _____ and call letters, _____ that was monitored by agency headquarters.

—Gates (numbers) were secured by security personnel.

—Winds at this time were beginning to increase in speed, causing unscheduled security alarms that were routinely investigated.

0855—(Name) briefed (name) on the status of preparations that had been completed.

0900—A communications link through the ARES (Amateur Radio Emergency Services) met with the state police (location), and the state armory in (location) (Governor's Command Center) was established and confirmed.

0945—(Name) was designated the onsite emergency director after (name) departed.

0958—Security was advised, via the hotline, that the (regulatory agency) high frequency radio was offline and that notification of its return to service would be made. (No such notification was ever received.)

1000—A briefing was held in (location) for all personnel remaining onsite. The emergency plan was reviewed, an accurate head count was obtained, emergency response/damage control teams were designated and individual responsibilities were assigned in the following areas: communication and coordination, manpower accountability, contingency equipment and supplies (nonsecurity), food/water/sanitation, and documentation. (Location) was designated the *secondary* location for a command post (CP) while (location) was designated the primary CP location.

—Two additional fire brigade personnel were called in pursuant to a request from (name) and asked to report to the facility. (They did so at 1100.)

1009—Phone check was made. Everything was O.K.

1025—An unconfirmed report was received that a state of emergency was declared by the governor, and as a result all roads were closed. This later proved to be an erroneous report.

1026—Portable HAM unit dispatched from (location) to the state police due to the unavailability of the original operator assigned to that location.

1030—An unconfirmed report was received that a tornado warning was in effect until 1800. (This was later confirmed.)

1031—Numerous power fluctuations were experienced and caused several supervisory alarms.

1045—(Regulatory agency) response center called to confirm status codes and was given an update on the company's status.

1100—Radio codes and appropriate telephone extensions were distributed to all onsite, nonsecurity personnel to facilitate internal communications.

—Emergency generators were started in anticipation of power outages.

—Additional fire brigade personnel, called in at 1000, arrived onsite.

1105—HAM operator links confirmed with (regulatory agencies).

—Storm was increasing in intensity.

1108—Emergency services group pager test was conducted.

1130—A report was received that the local fire/rescue dispatch center was operating on emergency power.

1145—Some power to (location) was shut down due to fluctuations.

1205—Additional power to (location) was shut down to stop numerous false and/or nuisance alarms.

1213—A weather report was received from HAM operator (name, location) who was linked to the NHC. It stated that winds were sustained at 120 mph.

1214—Power losses were reported in (locations).

1215—NHC Advisory 43 was received. It confirmed 1213 entry.

—Rounds of buildings were made by maintenance personnel.

1220—Power loss was reported at (location).

—Fans were turned off in (location).

—Exhaust system was turned off in (location).

1221—Power loss was reported in (location).

1225—Wind was gusting to ± 60 mph at this time; there were extensive outages and trees down in the area; the full impact of storm was expected by 1500.

1229—The eye of storm was reported over (location).

1235—Purchased power to facilities was lost.

—Diesel fire pump was started.

1239—A vent cover was blown from (location).

1240—Vacuum and cooling systems were shut down by maintenance personnel.

1245—A report received that local nuclear power plants went through shutdown procedures.

1300—Radio check. Everything was O.K.

—The emergency services group monitored the air system in (location).

1301—A power loss reported in (location).

1302—The eye of storm was reported over (location).

1310—The security response team was activated, equipped, and placed on standby.

1316—(Name) bridge, (location), was reported closed.

1320—Incoming phone service was lost.

1330—(Regulatory agency) response center was advised of company's status.

—Temporary lighting was placed in (location).

—(Name) bridge, (location), was reported closed.

1335—All onsite personnel were accounted for.

—Winds estimated at 75 to 80 mph with gusts estimated to 90 mph at facility. Full impact of storm was experienced.

1400—Hurricane was reported moving at 40 mph.

1406—Radio check. Everything was O.K.

1412—Shed near (location) was blown over; sections of sheet metal were blown away.

1417—An audible alarm was received from the computer room. The fire protection system was signaling trouble (due to loss of power). This was checked by (name), electronics maintenance, and (name). A fire watch every half hour was initiated and extra attention was given to main fire alarm panel.

1425—The storm was reported between (location) and (location), moving northeast, weakening rapidly.

1435—Emergency generators were checked by maintenance personnel. Everything was O.K.

1440—A small shed was blown over.

—A report was received that the storm had passed over this area and was into (location).

Actions after the Storm

(Date—Day 1)

1452—Additional damage reports were received: a portable guardhouse over-turned, limbs down in the vicinity of the northeast corner of the main parking lot, limbs down on the fence near (location), and a large tree down blocking the access road to (location). Repairs were initiated and are continuing.

1535—HAM coverage was set up for the second shift.

—A check of the onsite windspeed indicator showed it had stopped at 1235. The highest windspeed recorded at that time was approximately 55 to 60 mph.

1545—Per (local utility company, name), power will not be restored soon (possibly not for two to three days) due to the extensive damage.

1550—A report was received that the tornado warning was still in effect.

1613—A damage assessment was made; other than that previously noted, no additional damage was observed.

1645—The facility reverted to normal operations. (Regulatory agency) response center was advised. Extra security personnel to be released at the rate of (number/interval). At least (number) security guards were scheduled to remain onsite to augment regular second shift coverage.

—The fire watch on the computer room was continuing.

1700—It was decided by (name) that all emergency services personnel would be released at 1800 after their equipment was secured.

1730—(Estimated)—The in-house telephone system and its air conditioning unit was supplied with emergency power by facilities maintenance personnel.

1736—Security personnel were advised that the alert status had been down-graded.

—Efforts to contact (local power utility) for restoration of power con-tinued.

1740—(Estimated)—The diesel fire pump was turned off and checked by fire brigade personnel.

1749—(Local utility) was working on pole near (location).

1800—(Estimated)—Emergency services personnel were released.

—Repair and restoration efforts by maintenance personnel were con-tinuing.

—(Name) left the site.

—Electronics maintenance personnel on call were:

(list)

1830—Purchased power was restored.

1900—Repair and restoration efforts by maintenance personnel were con-tinuing.

2037—Per security shift supervisor normal operating mode was in effect.

(Date—Day 2)

Diverse—Power fluctuations were experienced during the day as repairs and restoration efforts were being made in the area.
   —Periodic status checks were made of facility by (name). No problems were reported.
   —Decision was made by (names) to resume normal operations beginning with third shift on (date).
   —The telephone system and its air conditioning unit returned to service.

(Date—Day 3)

There was nothing significant to report.

(Date—Day 4)

1000—(Various locations) were inspected for damage; none was found.
1030—(Regulatory agency) was informed of the company's return to normal operations.
1345—(Regulatory agency) was informed of the company's return to normal operations.

(Date—Day 5)

1330—A meeting was held to review this after-action report for completeness and accuracy. In attendance were:

(list)

Conclusion/Observations/Recommendations

In conclusion, the company was well prepared to deal with Hurricane (name). This was due largely to the dedication of the personnel involved in all phases of planning, preparation, response, and recovery. Their efforts were commendable; their cooperation, exemplary. Special mention should be made of:

(list)

and those involved in recovery/restoration operations without whose cooperation, facility response would have fallen far short.

Based on this experience, certain observations can be made, and consideration should be given them in the future. They are listed below, not in any particular order or priority.

1.   Weather advisories were obtained from the NWS and/or the NHC. While the information was accurate, often it was too late to help in the decision-making process, particularly regarding plant closings and shift cancellations. It should be noted that the decision to monitor one weather reporting source was sound. Therefore, consideration should

be given to establishing a liaison with meteorologists at one local TV and one local radio station and to basing weather-subject decisions on their forecasts. The NWS and, as appropriate, the NHC forecasts can continue to be monitored. In any event, information on weather should be obtained from a limited number of sources on a constant and consistent basis.

2. Although the manpower situation was favorably resolved, emergency response personnel could have been identified and alerted sooner, and coordination, initiated earlier.

3. Additional personnel should be assigned to the emergency response organization to handle routine tasks such as answering telephones and maintaining journals. In this case, the company was fortunate to have had some of its employees volunteer to perform these functions.

4. References for use in emergencies should be periodically updated and made more inclusive (as inclusive as possible) to assist with planning, preparation, response, and recovery efforts. Rather than grouping emergencies by nature or type, consideration should be given to grouping contingencies based on the amount of warning or advanced notice the company can reasonably expect (wherever possible). For example, in the case of a hurricane, advanced notice can reasonably be anticipated and an appropriate response formulated into a procedure. Events that can occur without warning, for example, a tornado, can be addressed in a separate procedure.

5. Decisions affecting production *and* the personnel department should be made jointly by their respective managements. In cases involving an impact on individual employees as was the case with Hurricane (name), due consideration should be given to employees' personal concerns, for example, damage to their homes, when deciding on appropriate courses of action. If employees are, as an additional example, in an evacuation zone, they should be allowed to disregard radio announcements to the effect that the plant is in operation.

6. Whatever the decision to be communicated to employees, a designated individual should be the *only* one to communicate with employees or offsite media. If the decision to close the plant or cancel specific shifts is made, it should be unqualified whenever possible so that the on-duty security supervisor can inform employees who subsequently arrive onsite. If certain employees are essential even though a shift has been cancelled, this should be communicated to security supervision so their access can be allowed. In this case, many employees who had not heard that normal operations would resume only on (date) with the third shift arrived and were informed that the plant was closed until that time. Several insisted that they were scheduled to work in spite of the announcement.

7. More coordination and subsequent communication regarding plant closings and/or shift cancellations at sister facilities is necessary so as

not to impact on this facility's security operations negatively. During the hours of 0500 to 0700, (day), (date), almost 150 telephone calls were received from employees requesting this facility's status.

Admittedly, looking at events in retrospect gives the viewer a clear and undistorted picture. Decisions that are made, often in seconds, are all too often scrutinized in the luxury of a calm, unpressured, after-the-fact atmosphere. No attempt is made here to do that; as with any critique, lessons learned can be put to good use in the future.

Appendixes

Appended to this report would be I) a listing of advisories from the National Hurricane Center and II) a copy of the (company) emergency plan for Hurricane (name) on (date).

D

Sample Event-Specific Plan

(NAME OF EVENT)
(DATE)
SECURITY PLAN

Prepared

Approved

Date

Distribution:

Contents

Access Control

1. Guests/visitors will enter through the main doors on (street) and be issued appropriate badges in the lobby/foyer area.
2. Guests/visitors in military or police uniforms will be checked but may not be issued a badge.
3. Caterers will enter initially through the main doors and be issued appropriate badges and then be directed to use the (street) entrance (which will be opened and staffed by security commencing at 1300).
4. Media representatives will be directed by signs on (street) to enter through the (street) entrance where a company management media liaison will meet them. Credentials (badges) will be issued at this location.
    Some media representatives, those without heavy equipment, will enter through the main entrance but will be accompanied by a company media liaison.
5. An entry will be made on the visitors log by security to the effect that the attached list of guests visited the facility in conjunction with the (special event). Lists to be attached to the visitors logs will be provided by (name/title).
6. No one other than *invited* guests/visitors will be admitted to the facility from 1400 through the conclusion of the affair.
7. Authorized badges for the event are shown below. No other badge will authorize the bearer access. Each badge is reproduced smaller than actual size and those showing a circle in the upper right corner will bear a unique stamp in that location.
8. Cameras and tape recorders will be allowed. Firearms and other items normally prohibited will not be allowed. Police officers, however, will be allowed to carry their weapons into the facility.

Access Control (Authorized Badges)

VIPs (blue)

Daily visitors (red)

Media (beige)

Guests (beige)

Caterers (beige)

Employees (blue or brown)

Agenda

1000	Welcome	(Name/title)
1030	Tour of facilities at (location)	(Name/title)
1200	Lunch at (location)	(Name/title)

Agenda

1400	Tour of facilities at (location)	(Name/title)
1530	Presentation ceremony	(Names/titles)
1600	Reception	(Name/title)

Chain of Command (Security)

(Place Organization Chart Here)

Command Posts (CPs)

1. The primary CP will be located at (location) security control center.
2. The CP is to be staffed by one uniformed officer, one plainclothes officer, and one stenographer.
3. Communications will be via two-way radio ([number] nets) and telephone.
4. CCTV surveillance will be maintained.
5. A secondary (backup) CP will be established in a security patrol vehicle that will be equipped with two-way radio and telephonic communications systems. It will also provide patrol and surveillance support.

Communications

1. The two-way radio frequency for the event is (frequency). The secondary frequency is (frequency).
2. Security will use frequency number 1 and monitor frequency number 2.
3. (Title) and (title) will communicate directly with sector supervisors only who will in turn relay or confirm messages. Call signs for (location) and (location) base stations will remain the same, that is, (call sign) and (call sign).
4. Special radio call signs are:

Red sector supervisor	(Call sign)
Orange sector supervisor	(Call sign)
Yellow sector supervisor	(Call sign)
Blue sector supervisor	(Call sign)
Team members	Last names

5. Radio communications are to be kept to a minimum; telephone or personal contact is to be used for routine messages whenever possible.
6. From 1530 until conclusion of event, the internal paging system will be turned off at the CP.
7. If an emergency evacuation is ordered (evacuation can only be ordered by [title] or [title]), the in-house fire alarm will be activated and an announcement to evacuate will be made over the internal paging system by security personnel from the CP.
8. Routine telephone calls to the company will be handled by regular switchboard operators and/or the (location) security control center.

Contingency Maintenance Support

1.   (Name), maintenance supervisor, will be equipped with a belt pager. If so directed, the CP will activate his or her pager by dialing (number).
2.   Upon receipt of a page, (name) will proceed directly to the CP.

Coordination with Local Law Enforcement Authorities (LLEA)

1.   Contact has been established and will be maintained with (name[s] of police departments and/or special police units and liaison[s] therein).
2.   (Name) police department patrol/traffic division will designate (street locations) as "No Parking" zones.

Coordination with Landlord

1.   The landlord (name), will be requested to secure the (street) entrance and/or allow posting of a security officer at that location. Additional parking spaces will be provided by (name) at (location[s]).

Crowd Control

1.   Crowd control is to be handled by company management escorts. (Escorts are to be briefed.)
2.   In the event of an emergency evacuation, security personnel will assist with evacuation via the closest exits.
3.   Security personnel will ensure that visitors/guests and employees do not exit the facility at other than authorized exits.
     a.   The authorized exit for employees, media, and caterers is via the (street) exit, (location) to be manned by security at 1300.
     b.   The authorized exit for visitors is via the main entrance at the security control center.
4.   Security personnel will be alert for thefts or attempted thefts, suspicious persons, unusual circumstances or activity, and suspicious packages or parcels.
5.   *All* persons must clear a metal detector upon exit. Exceptions can be authorized by the following persons *only:*
                                   (list)

Escort Instructions

1.   Brief the group that is being escorted on:
     a.   Security
          1)   Do not touch operating machines or handle anything without the escort's approval.
          2)   Do not deviate from the tour route.
          3)   The normal safety glasses requirement has been waived for tours (except for tours to operating areas). The normal safety shoe requirement has also been waived.

      4)   If emergency evacuation is necessary, the closest emergency exits will be used.

2.   Escorts are responsible for their groups' compliance with all safety and security rules, requirements and procedures, and emergency evacuation of the group if necessary.

Emergency Evacuation

1.   The internal fire alarm and/or a P.A. announcement will be used to signal an emergency evacuation.
2.   Emergency evacuation can be ordered only by (title) or (title).
3.   Escorts will evacuate their groups; security personnel will assist.
4.   Evacuation will take place via the closest emergency exit.
5.   Sector supervisors will be responsible for unlocking additional exits if necessary.
6.   Potential causes for evacuation include (not in priority):
    A.   Verified bomb threat
    B.   Fire
    C.   Explosion

Executive Protection

1.   Plainclothes security personnel and sector supervisors will assume additional responsibility of providing extra attention to and protecting VIPs in their sectors.

Fire Department Support

1.   The (name) fire department has been advised of event and will provide support.

Firearms Passes

1.   Passes authorizing designated (and permitted) security personnel will be issued. A sample will be posted at each security control center.

Firstaid/Medical

1.   An R.N. and/or an M.D. should be stationed in the medical department during an event.
2.   (Name), police department ambulance service to be advised and asked to provide immediate response.

Intelligence

1.   A liaison should be established with the local law enforcement authorities.
2.   Intelligence estimates will be made prior to this event to ascertain, if possible, if any unauthorized activity is anticipated that would involve company personnel or this event.

Jeopardies/Risks

1. The following jeopardies/risks exist (not in order of priority):
   a. Violent or nonviolent protests (and/or forcible intrusions)
   b. Covert intrusions ("gate crashers")
   c. Bomb threats
   d. Bombing
   e. Assassinations or attempts at such
   f. Normal emergencies, accidents, and illnesses
   g. Other

Media Relations

1. One (company) management person should be assigned to maintain liaison with the media, expedite their entry and exit, and facilitate their movements within the facility.
2. A press conference will be held for media in the conference room at 1445 hours. The press will be taken on a tour *after* the ceremony.

Notifications

1. The following federal, state, and local agencies will be advised of the event:

(list)

Personnel

Staffing: (Number) of uniformed personnel ([number] additional)
                (Number) of plainclothes personnel
Deployment: (See also attached diagram)
                (List deployment positions)
Instructions: 1. Deter/prevent theft/diversion
                2. Monitor crowd for suspicious activity/persons
                3. Assist visitors
                4. Assist with evacuation if necessary
                5. Respond, as directed, to emergencies/incidents
                6. Protect VIPs if necessary
                7. Authorize use of firearms only to protect self or another from use of deadly physical force.

Special
instructions   1. Familiarize self with assigned area, methods of communication, normal exits, and emergency exits
                2. Exterior posts/patrols to be alert for protestors and/or vehicles.

(Place deployment diagram here)

Postevent Instructions

1. Conduct a thorough search of interior and exterior premises for persons, packages, and so forth.

2.   Lock and secure all entrances and activate alarms.
     a.   Conduct an alarm survey of all perimeter entrances.
3.   Make a final check of parking lots, adjacent streets, and so forth.

Prohibited Items

1.   Cameras and tape recorders will be allowed.
2.   All other normally prohibited items, for example, firearms and/or ammunition will not be allowed except for firearms and ammunition carried by onduty police officers.

Publicity

1.   Publicity prior to the event will be kept to the absolute minimum.
2.   Media representatives will be invited two days before the event (on or about [date]).
3.   Media representatives include:

                              (list)

Recordkeeping

1.   A stenographer will be assigned to the CP to initiate and maintain necessary documentation.
2.   A chronological synopsis of the event will be prepared for an after-action report and debriefing.
3.   An after-action report will be prepared by (name/title) and will include the chronological synopsis referred to above and a critique of the security operation. A debriefing will be scheduled and conducted by (name/title).

Safety Procedures

1.   Normal safety glasses and footwear requirements will be waived for the event except for tours/visits to operating areas. In those cases, safety glasses will be required.
2.   An extra supply of safety glasses will be available at each security control center; however, it will be an escort's responsibility to request them for his or her group.
3.   Tour groups must not deviate from the main aisles during their visit.
4.   All escorts and security personnel will be familiar with all emergency exits and routes.

Shuttle Vehicles

1.   Shuttle vehicles will pick up and discharge passengers at the main entrances.
2.   Vehicles will park at (location[s]).
3.   Special dashboard placards may be issued for shuttle vehicles; samples will be posted at the security control centers.

Preevent Instructions

1. A complete search of the (location) facility, interior and exterior, will be made at 0630 hours on (date). The second shift security officers will be held over to assist.
2. Prior to assuming a post, each security officer will check his or her assigned area for anything unusual.

Miscellaneous Instructions

1. (Name/title) will post notices pertaining to parking spaces being reserved for the event and advising employees to exit through the (street) entrance after 1300 hours.
2. (Number) [security] officers will be detailed to the shuttle and can provide security for VIPs at the luncheon scheduled for (title) at (location).

E

Sample
Crisis Management Plan

**(COMPANY)
CRISIS MANAGEMENT PLAN**

Prepared:

Reviewed:

Approved:

Contents

Introduction

This plan has been developed for the safety and welfare of all employees. The actions outlined herein must be followed by every employee and visitor to enable the appropriate response to, and ultimate recovery from, an emergency, crisis, or contingency that threatens or could threaten personnel or property. Compliance with this plan, therefore, is mandatory for all employees or visitors. The basic action that must be taken by *every* employee upon becoming aware of a crisis or potential crisis is to notify the Security Department immediately at (location, phone number).

Definitions and Abbreviations

I. Definitions

Action	The doing of something; performing a task. Used to describe a task based on a particular decision.
Assessment	The verification that an emergency situation exists and the determination of the potential or actual consequences and the proper response(s) required.
Assessment actions	Actions taken during or after a contingency to obtain and process information necessary for making decisions to implement specific measures.
Contingency	An event that is of possible but uncertain occurrence; something that is liable to happen as an adjunct to something else.
Continuing emergency	Site or general emergencies that continue for one hour or longer.
Corrective actions	Measures taken to terminate, or counteract the effects of, a crisis or emergency situation.
Crisis	An unstable or crucial time or state of affairs the outcome of which will make a decisive difference for better or worse.
Crisis control center	The location from where crisis will be managed by the crisis management director and team.
Crisis management director	The person who is responsible for assessment of crises, emergencies, and contingencies and has operational control of all personnel involved in recovery operations.
Crisis management plan	A specific plan designed to describe the decisions, actions, and responsibilities related to a contingency affecting the facility or its personnel.
Crisis management team	A group of personnel that provides the president and the crisis management director with information and assistance relative to a contingency.

Criteria	Standards, rules, or tests upon which a decision can be based.
Drill	A strictly supervised, repetitive instruction period aimed at perfecting skills in a particular operation. A drill is often a component of an exercise.
Exercise	An event that tests a major portion of the basic elements within a crisis management plan or organization in order to demonstrate and/or refine preparedness.
Recovery	Restoration of the facility and personnel to a normal (precrisis) condition.

II. Abbreviations (Acronyms)

(List as applicable)

Scope and Applicability

I. General

ABC Industries, a division of XYZ Incorporated, is a manufacturing enterprise with facilities in (locations). Commercial widgets are produced in (locations) and military widgets are produced in (locations). In general, the processes involved at ABC Division facilities are typical of those usually associated with similar manufacturing industries, that is, machining, polishing, woodworking, and so forth. The only factor that could increase the normal potential magnitude of any crisis, emergency, or contingency would be the presence of assembled widgets in substantial quantities.

II. Scope

This crisis management plan contains the policy and a generalized description of personnel, programs, equipment, and outside agency assistance that together comprise ABC's response to crisis situations. This plan is designed to complement the normal operation of the division and does *not* supersede normal operating procedures until a crisis situation occurs.

The life-preserving and safety provisions contained herein supersede security requirements to the extent that security of personnel and property is a secondary consideration whenever a period of potential danger to life or limb exists. While the safeguarding of personnel and property is of secondary concern, however, it is still of major critical importance.

The (title) normally directs physical security efforts during a crisis and/or emergency. He or she has authority to stop egress from the division facilities except where personal safety or injury or potential thereof are involved. The saving of lives and the protection of personnel prevail in the event that this plan conflicts with any other plan, policy, or procedure.

This plan shall prevail during crisis or emergencies on division property.

III. Applicability

Compliance with this plan is *mandatory* for all personnel entering ABC property or facilities.

Summary of Crisis Management Plan

I. General

Crisis conditions that could occur at ABC can be grouped into six basic categories, as outlined in the next section (Emergency/Crisis Conditions), and include (in order of increasing severity):

A. Personnel emergencies
B. Emergency alerts
C. Localized emergencies
D. Plant emergencies
E. Site emergencies
F. General emergencies

II. A Typical Emergency Scenario

Word of a potential crisis—for example, fire, tornado, or gas leak—is received during normal operating hours. A determination is made that personnel are in jeopardy and evacuation is ordered. Employees assemble at predesignated assembly points and a head count is initiated. First aid commences as soon as it is required and notification is made to appropriate agencies and personnel. A crisis control center (CCC) is activated and crisis management team (CMT) personnel are assembled. Preparations for rescue and/or reentry are made. The security force establishes perimeter protection to prevent the general public and employees from approaching the facility, to prevent theft of product, and to assist responding agencies and personnel. Appropriate measures are instituted to overcome the crisis. The crisis management plan will remain in effect until the facility is reoccupied.

Emergency/Crisis Conditions

I. Personnel Emergencies

Personnel emergencies consist of any injury resulting from an accident or other occurrence onsite. Personnel emergencies normally do not activate the CMT; however, they may require local ambulance or medical services. All personnel injuries must be reported to the (title).

Personnel emergencies are classified in order of increasing severity:

A. *Extremely minor injuries.* The injured persons are capable of administering first aid to themselves and returning to work immediately; the injury does not require professional medical attention. This type of injury does not activate the CMT. Examples include minor cuts, bumps, and bruises.

B.   *Minor injuries,* patient is ambulatory and capable of evacuating him- or herself for any necessary medical evaluation. The injured person may return to work or depart the area for medical evaluation. This type of injury does not activate the CMT; however, the patient may require assistance in administering first aid. Such assistance is usually supplied by onsite trained medical personnel or security personnel trained in first aid. Examples of this type of injury include minor acid or alcohol burns (restricted to a small area of the body), contusions, lacerations, or sprains requiring medical evaluation.

C.   *Serious injuries* and the patient is ambulatory. Attendance as for (B) above except the patient will receive assisted evacuation for additional evaluation. Serious lacerations requiring several stitches, contusions, or sprains incapacitating individuals to the extent the patient must be accompanied to a medical facility for additional evaluation, acid or alkaline burns covering a large portion of the body, suspected fractures leaving the patient ambulatory, someone rendered unconscious (but revived), electric shock, and exposure to toxic fumes or gases are examples of ambulatory serious injuries.

D.   *Severe, serious injuries patient not ambulatory.* This necessitates outside medical evacuation assistance. This type of injury will probably activate a first aid team, which will administer immediate first aid and prepare the victim for evacuation. Arterial bleeding, serious acid or alkaline burns, broken legs, and unconscious patients are examples of this type of injury.

E.   *Additional personnel crises.* Threats, expressed or implied, to any employee where the objective is to force ABC or XYZ Incorporated to follow a course of action not of its choosing, will cause activation of the CMT. Examples include kidnapping, hostage situations, and violent acts or threats thereof. In any such case, the CMT will be activated by the (title) or higher authority upon the recommendation of the (title).

II. Emergency Alerts

This classification of emergency involves specific situations that create a hazard potential that was previously nonexistent or latent. No damage to the facility has occurred nor have any personnel within the facility been harmed. These situations are not serious enough in nature to declare a higher state of emergency; however, they do require evaluation, special equipment, or special operations to preclude escalation to a higher state of alert. Emergency alerts include responses to:

A.   *Natural phenomena such as severe weather and earthquakes.* Examples of this type of emergency alert are lightning striking the facilities, 12 inches of snow in less than a 24-hour period, tornado or hurricane alert announced for the area by the national weather service, an ice storm that causes the loss of electricity, and earth tremors registering one to three on the Richter Scale.

B. *Fire in a protected area.* Examples of this type of emergency alert are small controllable fires within 1000 feet, but not closer than 25 feet, of the facilities and an uncontrolled fire more than 1000 feet from the facilities.

C. *Certain security breaches.* Examples of this type of emergency alert are the receipt of a bomb threat, two or more persons initiating an organized demonstration on company property, or any civil disturbance occurring on adjacent public property.

D. *Miscellaneous occurrences.* Examples of this type of alert are unexpected release of toxic gases or liquids, loss of commercially furnished electricity for more than 30 minutes, two or more serious injuries occurring simultaneously, or any unsafe situation not previously described that requires special evaluation.

III. Localized Emergencies

This classification involves abnormal conditions, restricted to a small portion of the facility, that do not interfere with overall operation of the facility. This type of emergency will not activate the CMT. The situation will normally be neutralized by operator-immediate actions; however, certain specialized assistance (depending on the situation) may be required. Small explosions, isolated equipment malfunctions, failure of electrical circuits, and spills are examples of localized emergencies.

IV. Plant Emergencies

This classification involves severe damage or threat of severe damage to facilities. It requires an evaluation to determine how the situation can be neutralized without escalation to a higher emergency classification.

A plant emergency will most likely be caused by natural phenomena (severe weather or earthquake), security breach (sabotage, civil disturbance, or bomb threat), and fires outside the facilities. The following are examples of this type of emergency:

A. Natural phenomena causing:
    1. Uncontrolled release of toxic gases or liquids
    2. Damage to a waste holding system that may allow pollution to occur
    3. Damage to the manufacturing area exhaust system, such as roof ventilation structures having panels or guy wires broken or missing

B. Security breaches such as:

    1.   A successful act of sabotage
    2.   A disturbance involving ten or more people
    3.   A bomb threat determined to be authentic
C.   Fires located:
    1.   Closer than 25 feet to or in a building
    2.   Controllable fires within buildings that can easily be extinguished with emergency equipment

V. Site Emergencies

This classification of emergency involves a situation that is an immediate threat to the life or safety of persons inside the facilities. Most site emergencies will result in an immediate or eventual evacuation from the facilities. Site emergencies can result from a security breach, a natural phenomenon, or a fire that engulfs a building or buildings.

    Examples of site emergencies are:

A.   A successful act of sabotage causing severe damage to facilities
B.   A covert armed attack
C.   A tank or pipe within a building that ruptures (and the resulting leak cannot be controlled)
D.   Severe damage to division facilities
E.   A major fire that renders the facility untendable

VI. General Emergencies

This classification of emergency involves any situation that poses a substantial safety hazard to those persons residing immediately adjacent to company property. The likelihood of occurrence of an emergency of this sort is extremely low.

    A general emergency might occur if two catastrophic natural phenomena occurred almost simultaneously. An example would be an earthquake (Richter 6–10) immediately followed by a hurricane (winds greater than 75 miles per hour), a tornado, or a flood.

    A general emergency could occur, for example, if the facility were captured and held hostage by a terrorist group that announced they possessed enough of the correct materials to blow up the facility.

VII. Spectrum of Postulated Accidents

When the above is taken into consideration, the summary analysis of the emergency classes and the postulated accidents indicate the following implications for emergency planning: (1) assessment of offsite impact, (2) instrumentation capability for prompt detection, and (3) continued assessment and manpower needs. The results of the summary analysis are contained in Table 1.

Table 1 Postulated Accident Summary Analysis

Type of Emergency	Offsite Impact	Instrumentation Capability	Assessment and Manpower Needs
Personnel emergency	Ambulance, medical, and hospital support	Not applicable in this case	Manpower exists onsite to administer first aid.
	Local law enforcement authorities (LLEA) assistance		Offsite medical assistance may be required depending on the extent of the injury.
Emergency alert	LLEA for bomb threats, civil disturbances, and serious labor disputes	VHF-FM weather monitor	Required manpower is normally present during daytime operating shifts.
	Fire department for fires		Certain personnel such as department managers and maintenance may be called in during other shifts or on offshifts.
			Public utility and contract maintenance services may have to be requested for more complicated repairs or assessment.
Localized emergency	No offsite impact expected	Assessment is observational in nature	Immediate operator assessment and corrective actions should be able to neutralize this type of emergency. The assistance of maintenance personnel and equipment may be necessary.
		Not applicable in this case	

Type of Emergency	Offsite Impact	Instrumentation Capability	Assessment and Manpower Needs
Plant emergency	LLEA, fire department, ambulance, medical, or hospital assistance	Assessment is observational in nature Not applicable in this case	This facility does not maintain the expertise to evaluate or repair the damage related to a plant emergency. This means outside contractor assistance will be requested. Corporate representatives may evaluate the situation and eventual manpower requirements could be a result of the evaluation. These actions are expected to receive the concurrence of federal, state, and local agencies.
Site or general emergency	LLEA assistance Fire department assistance (if necessary) Ambulance, medical, or hospital assistance Regulatory agencies' services (if an actual event) Corporate assistance (Public safety and relations will be of major concern)	As appropriate to situation	Actual site emergency will require maximum assistance available from corporate, federal, state, and local agencies.

Organizational Control for Emergencies/Crises

Organizational control begins prior to the occurrence of an emergency as emergency-related planning and training responsibilities are assigned to certain job positions within the normal plant organization.

I. Normal Plant Organization

The (location) of ABC Industries does not operate continuously. It usually operates one daily operational shift (0800–1600). There are several persons working in the (location) area around the clock. The remaining staff work week shifts, and weekend shifts are normally offshifts. This results in one basic shift organization (consult current organizational charts).

The (location) plant usually operates three daily operational shifts (0800–1600, 1600–2400, and 2400–0800) Monday through Friday. The remaining weekend shifts are normally offshifts. This results in three basic shift organizations (consult current organizational charts).

Preparation for unforeseen emergency situations is normally accomplished by the (location) day shift organization.

Preparation is facilitated by assigning, planning, and training. Assignments are:

(list)

The (title) assures that (1) a crisis management plan and program are in place and (2) directs or assigns the direction of the investigation in the event of a major or continuing site or general emergency.

The (title) assists the (title) as directed and is responsible for providing technical advice and assistance to the overall emergency planning effort. He or she ensures that at least one individual trained to administer first aid is assigned to each security workshift and also that all security personnel complete prescribed emergency training.

Other personnel may be assigned as necessary and shall be trained accordingly and periodically participate in reinforcement training and drills.

II. Onsite Emergency Organization

The onsite emergency organization for most personnel emergencies, emergency alerts, and localized emergencies is identical to the normal organization. Plant emergencies (other than security, which activate certain specific procedures) will normally be evaluated and neutralized by the production organization according to its procedures.

Site or general emergencies (other than security) and some personnel emergencies will initiate the shift emergency organization. It is expected that the emergency organizations may gradually be augmented by employee recall if necessary.

A.   *Direction and coordination*

The (title) is responsible for all operations on company property during a crisis or emergency and has the authority necessary for directing all actions within that boundary. The (title) reports to the (title), and will hereafter be referred to as the crisis management director (CMD).

The CMD is responsible for (1) taking charge in the event of a crisis or emergency; (2) ensuring that immediate action is initiated; (3) determining the authenticity of any threat; (4) notifying federal, state, and local government authorities; (5) beginning plans for recovery from the emergency; (6) recovering the facility and restoring it to normal operation; and (7) initiating formal reports. The CMD retains these responsibilities until relieved by the (title) or higher authority. All company personnel shall follow the directions of the CMD and the CMT (through the CMD).

A CMT shall be formed to assist the CMD in fulfilling his or her responsibilities. The purpose of this team is to provide the CMD with technical advice and support and to accomplish time-consuming coordination with outside agencies. The team will also provide these services to the (title). The CMT shall normally assemble in the conference (board) room and consist of:

1.   (Title)
2.   (Title)
3.   (Title)
4.   (Title)
5.   (Title)

The *(title)* will serve as chairman of the CMT and advise the CMD accordingly. He or he shall prepare or approve reports required by and prepared for the various regulatory agencies and the news media.

The *(title[s])* will provide technical evaluation and assistance during all crises and emergencies.

The *(title)* will determine the financial impact of a crisis or emergency and assist in its evaluation. He or she will also initiate and maintain a record of the incident.

B.   *Plant staff emergency assignments*

A site or general emergency may necessitate the plant staff being assigned to certain functional areas by the CMD. These assignments will be determined at the time they become necessary.

III. Augmentation of Onsite Emergency Operations

Augmentation of onsite or general emergency operations can be separated into two support categories.

A.   *Corporate support*

This facility maintains the equipment and personnel necessary to deal with most crises or emergencies. It is stored for the most part in security control centers at (location).

[Public relations and safety assistance can be provided by corporate headquarters at (location).] It is also expected that supporting personnel from other corporate organizations could be used to augment company personnel to provide 24-hour coverage during a continuing emergency.

The notification of governmental authorities and release of information to news media, in coordination with governmental authorities, will be controlled by (title) or a higher authority.

B.   *Outside services support*

Outside services and agencies that can be expected to render support (as necessary) include:

(List all such services and agencies)

Emergency telephone numbers are maintained by security control centers.

Emergency Measures

I. Activation of Emergency Organization

Personnel emergencies normally will not activate the CMT.

Emergency alerts normally will not activate the CMT. However, the alerts do require departmental evaluation to determine corrective actions and whether the situation requires escalation to the emergency level.

Localized emergencies normally will not activate the CMT. They will be neutralized or escalated into a higher state of emergency.

Plant emergencies normally will not automatically activate the CMT. Facility management is required to make a conscious decision, however, as to whether to activate the emergency organization or to escalate the level of emergency. Appropriate management notifications will be made in the event of a plant emergency.

Some personnel emergencies (as outlined earlier in Emergency/Crisis Conditions, Personnel Emergencies) will activate the CMT.

The occurrence of a site emergency automatically activates the CMT.

A general emergency will normally develop from an already existing site emergency, and the emergency organization will already have been activated. In any event, all general emergencies will activate the CMT.

The CMT or (title) will immediately notify the appropriate governmental agencies when a general emergency exists.

II. Assessment Actions

Personnel emergencies, emergency alerts, and localized emergencies do not require special assessment assistance such as structural contractors, electronics technicians, or other similar types of specialists. Initial assessment will be conducted by company employees. They will continue to assess the emergency until they determine that the situation is beyond their assessment capability. Assessment and requests for assistance from outside contractors will be made as necessary. Security breach assessments will be accomplished according to security plans and procedures. Fire assessments will be accomplished by the CMD or by appropriate company management personnel in the absence of the CMD.

Should any emergency continue for one hour or more, it is considered a continuing emergency. Call-in of offsite personnel to expand the crisis management organization may be required.

General emergency evaluation (if required) is expected to be an extension of an ongoing site emergency evaluation.

III. Corrective Actions

Personnel emergency patients will be administered first aid and evacuated for additional medical treatment as required.

Any civil disturbance, labor dispute, or bomb threat that results in an emergency alert will be corrected according to existing security department procedures. Normally, damages to the facility that cause an emergency alert will initially be evaluated by internal maintenance personnel. There may be occasions, however, when the corrective repairs will be beyond internal capability so that outside contractors will be requested.

Any damage resulting from a localized emergency will normally be repaired by maintenance personnel.

Conditions that cause a plant emergency normally cannot be completely neutralized by the personnel and equipment available. The initial evaluation and corrective actions will be begun by facility employees and outside assistance will be requested on an as-needed basis. Fires will be immediately fought by plant personnel, and offsite assistance will be requested if necessary. Security-related plant emergencies will be corrected in accordance with security department plans and procedures.

Site or general emergency initial corrective actions are similar. Hazardous zones that preclude entry without proper protective equipment shall be identified and clearly marked. The presence of toxic fumes that require breathing equipment, protective clothing, and other protective measures are typical examples.

Site or general emergencies resulting from natural phenomenon will be assessed after reentry has been approved. Damage of great magnitude may require product and/or equipment to be moved. Outside contractor assistance may be required to repair structural damage. Security breaches will be addressed and corrected. This type of emergency, if caused by a major fire, will normally be corrected by local firefighting support.

IV. Protective Actions

Immediate notification of onsite personnel that an emergency has occurred is accomplished by an automatic wailing siren alarm or by personnel announcement (P.A. system, in-plant telephone, or intercom). All visitors and contractors at the facility will be notified by their escorts. Notification of key management personnel on the plant site will be accomplished through one or more of the aforementioned systems. If they are not onsite, the (title), the (title), and the (title) will be notified as promptly as possible by telephone, radio, page, or courier. Other personnel will be notified as promptly as practicable by telephone, personal pager, or messenger if necessary. The CMD has authority to secure immediate medical, fire, and police assistance. Notification of other agencies is normally reserved for the (title) or a higher authority. The CMD, however, may initiate required notifications.

When personnel are found to be missing during the accounting process, the CMD must establish their whereabouts and determine whether emergency lifesaving rescue needs to be attempted. An accounting for missing or injured personnel is made immediately following an evacuation to a predetermined location. A visual check is conducted at the assembly point and then around the perimeter of the affected facility. If no hazards or toxic materials are found, the CMD may authorize entry into the plant to complete the survey or determine the location of the problem.

Rescue volunteers should be selected from those having had prior training (with the CMD not participating if any other persons familiar with rescue operations are present. If outside rescue services, for example, fire department personnel, are present), they should be used in conjunction with, or instead of, company employee volunteers.

Injured personnel will be identified during the accounting and their care and first aid will be given priority over all other action.

In the event of a site, or general, emergency nothing shall be removed or disturbed without permission of the CMD (or a designee), to protect against loss of material and information needed in an investigation. Appropriate inventories will be made and the necessary reports filed as specified.

The general public will be protected from accidental injury or exposure by blocking access to company property to all except authorized personnel.

Notification of corporate officials is reserved for the (title), (or, in his or her absence or inability to function, for the CMD).

An emergency telephone hot line at each facility is connected to the local police department. In addition, a two-way radio system and telephones are maintained at each security control center. The (titles) are also reachable through radio and/or signal paging equipment.

V. Aid to Affected Personnel

Persons injured in an emergency situation are promptly identified and segregated in terms of types of injury. Records are started immediately and are maintained under direction of the CMD (or a designee).

Adequate first aid supplies and facilities are maintained at both facilities to provide minimal required treatment.

Appropriate equipment and supplies suitable for dealing with emergencies are maintained at both facilities.

VI. Professional Medical Assistance

If possible, medical advice will be obtained from the local physician under contract to the company, or from other medical personnel, before transportation of any injured persons.

VII. Transportation of Injured

Local support agencies that may be called upon for transportation of injured personnel include all (location) area ambulance services and emergency response agencies.

VIII. Other

The security guard force may be expanded as needed by a request to the firm providing contract guard service. Additional staff and technical personnel are available from within (company name). Current listings (telephone lists) are available for use by the CMD.

Emergency Facilities and Equipment

I. Crisis Control Center

The initial assembly areas include the parking lots at each facility. If alternate areas are deemed necessary, a determination will be made at the time.

The crisis control centers are located at the appropriate security control centers and are equipped with:

A.   Commercial electricity
B.   Backup generator
C.   Emergency lights

II. Communications Systems

The crisis control centers are equipped with the following communications equipment:

A.   Commercial telephones
B.   Hot lines to the local police and fire departments
C.   High frequency FM radios
D.   FM radio scanners

III. First Aid and Medical Facilities

Standard first aid kits are located at each security control center. A fully equipped medical department is located at each division facility.

IV. Damage Control Equipment and Supplies

This division has limited damage control capability. Damage control beyond the in-house capability will be accomplished by contractors on an as-needed basis.

Maintaining Emergency Preparedness

I. Organizational Preparedness

All persons directly involved in the execution of the crisis management plan must complete four hours of initial training including (but not limited to):

A. Crisis/emergency operations
    1. Classification systems
    2. Organization
    3. Duties and responsibilities
    4. Safety
    5. Security
    6. Communications
    7. Responses
    8. Resources
B. Notification procedures
C. Assessment actions
D. Damage control
E. Fire prevention and incipient firefighting
    1. Equipment
    2. Resources

In addition, completion of one hour of reinforcement training annually is required.

Persons directly involved in the execution of the crisis management plan include (but are not limited to):

(list)

Representatives of the (name) department will meet annually with representatives of local support agencies (for example, police and fire departments) to renew mutual understanding of the role they play in neutralizing crisis/emergency situations at (company).

A site or general emergency exercise will be scheduled annually. The exercise scenario will be prepared from simulations of events which could occur at this facility. These exercises shall include the participation of employees assigned responsibilities for implementing this plan. The exercise will be coordinated with local and state agencies. The participation of local police, ambulance, civil defense, and fire agencies will be solicited. It is expected they will cooperate to the extent their schedules and budgets permit. As a minimum, the communication links and notification procedures to the agencies will be exercised.

The (title) is responsible for evaluating the exercise, soliciting feedback, identifying any weak points, and initiating any necessary improvement actions at the conclusion of each exercise.

II. Emergency Equipment and Supplies

The emergency equipment and supplies stored in the security control centers will be assessed for serviceability and inventoried once each quarter by a member of the security department.

Recovery

When a situation appears to be under control, a decision will be made by the CMD that reentry is safe. Actual reentry shall be made only with the express approval of the (title) or his designee.

Following a verified false alarm, operations may be resumed by authority of the CMD. Resumption of operations following a verified actual incident may be authorized only by the (title) or a higher authority.

Emergency equipment and supplies will be inspected and inventoried at the conclusion of an emergency. The equipment and supplies requiring cleaning or repair will be cleaned or repaired prior to storage. Equipment or supplies losing their utility during the emergency will be replaced.

Appendixes

Emergency Control Action Summary*

A. Ensure that the emergency is identified and that immediately needed action is taken (including evacuation and first aid if necessary).
B. Activate firefighting and rescue as necessary.
C. Establish a crisis control center based on existing conditions. Locations could include:
    1. Security control center(s)
    2. Board/conference room(s)
    3. Parking lot(s)
D. Establish and maintain a formal log of events.
E. Evacuate facilities or selected areas as necessary (decision to be made by the [title], the [title], or the CMD).
F. Establish appropriate in-plant and offsite communications.
G. Ensure that accurate personnel count is established.
H. Establish liaison with outside agencies (if any outside agencies are responding).
I. Ensure that appropriate company personnel have been notified.
J. Activate CMT if necessary.
K. Ensure that emergency care of personnel is initiated.
L. Evaluate extent of incident effect and damage.
M. Control reentry of evacuated facilities or areas.
N. Coordinate and direct in-plant emergency support services (including security personnel).
O. Contact offsite communication and media sources (limited to [title] or higher authority).
P. Priority of actions are:
    1. Protection and preservation of life and limb.
    2. Safeguarding classified data and/or material.
    3. Environmental protection.
    4. Protection of facilities, equipment and product.
    5. Restoration of normal operations.

Upon their arrival, the individuals holding the positions listed below will assume assigned responsibilities.

Responsibility	Assigned to
Safety, security, and communications	(Title)
Medical services	Plant physician or (title)
	Senior nurse or (title)

---

* Actions may be concurrent and are *not* all inclusive; as stated herein, they are merely guidelines to use in expediting a response.

Damage assessment and control	(Title)
Equipment shutdown	(Title)
Material handling	(Title)

Authority and Accountability

During a crisis/emergency the CMD is a direct agent of the (title) and has authority to direct, assign, and delegate all personnel and activities necessary to control the situation. Certain exceptions are listed below:

Specific Authority Withheld	Reserved For
Notification of regulatory agencies	(Title)
	(Title)
	(Title)
Contact with media	(Title)
	(Title)

Fire and/or Bombing, Explosion

Definition: Any fire/explosion that poses a threat to personnel or property.

Actions:
1. Summon fire department if necessary.
2. Evacuate affected areas and account for personnel.
3. Provide rescue and medical aid.
4. Evaluate likelihood of toxic chemical involvement.
5. Evaluate and minimize product hazard.
6. Shut off utility and service lines to area affected.
7. Advise CMD.

Power Outage

Definition: General power failure of facility lasting more than five minutes.

Actions:
1. Assemble CMT to extent needed.
2. Confirm manual switching to emergency power where necessary.
3. Evacuate people from dark areas or total evacuation of facilities.
4. Secure all controlled-access areas.
5. Instruct employees to remain at work stations unless otherwise directed.
6. Obtain information on duration of outage.
7. Advise offsite management personnel as necessary.
8. Order maintenance shutdown to reduce restarting load.
9. Decide on whether to hold employees or send them home.
10. Decide on succeeding shifts.

Actions: 11. Take any additional security measures.
(continued)   12. Provide restartup plans.

Civil Disturbance

Definition: Riot, protest assemblies, road blockage, or threatened or
                    attempted forcible entry to company property.
Actions: 1. Prepare security force.
                    2. Notify local police.
                    3. Check and periodically recheck all communications.
                    4. Barricade entrances to property (if appropriate).
                    5. Set up perimeter patrols if appropriate.
                    6. Set up guard mobilization if appropriate.
                    7. Notify management.
                    8. Decide on disposition of employees.
                       a.   Onsite
                       b.   Offsite

Bomb or Incendiary Threat

Definition: Notification that an explosive device is in plant.
Actions: 1. Alert security force and follow bomb threat standard
                       operating procedure (SOP).
                    2. Notify local police.
                    3. Establish validity of threat.
                    4. Establish the degree and timing of plant evacuation and
                       equipment/service shutdown if appropriate.
                    5. Evaluate shift change implications.
                    6. Advise (title[s]).
                    7. Barricade plant access.
                    8. Count personnel.
                    9. Initiate search plan.

Uncontrolled/Unscheduled Environmental Release

Definition: Release of chemicals that may present a hazard to persons,
                    animals, and/or the environment.
Actions: 1. Notify security.
                    2. Evacuate areas as required.
                    3. List areas affected.
                    4. Identify cause and sources.
                    5. Notify environmental engineering personnel.
                    6. Terminate release (if possible).
                    7. Provide for first aid/medical assistance.
                    8. Count personnel
                    9. Survey extent of release.
                    10. Notify management.

Actions: (continued)	11. Determine actual and potential effect on surrounding area and population.
	12. Notify outside agencies as appropriate.

Acts of Nature

Definition:	Nonplant initiated emergencies such as tornado or earthquake that cause or threaten physical damage to persons, plant, facilities, or services.
Actions:	1. Treat any injuries and provide ambulance/hospital services if necessary.
	2. Assemble CMT.
	3. Develop emergency plan.
	4. Implement emergency plan.
	5. Count personnel.
	6. Assess damage to plant security and alarm system.
	7. Correct damage to security and alarm system.
	8. Assess any effects on product.
	9. Check all communications systems.
	10. Notify corporate headquarters as necessary.
	11. Make recovery/reentry plans as necessary.

Call Sequence List

1. Security control centers (locations and numbers).
2. (Title)
3. (Title)
4. (Title)
5. (Title)
6. (Title)
7. (Title)

Fire Protection Plan

Introduction

The potential for loss of life from a fire at (company) is directly related to the fire hazard risk of our manufacturing operations and processes and the in-use or stored materials supporting these operations and processes. The only significant fuel available in this facility to support a major fire would be the petroleum-based cutting oils. As these oils are combustible rather than flammable, the risk of a life threatening fire is low. Obviously the use and storage of (item[s]) would, on the surface, constitute a life-threatening hazard. However, the quantities stored within the building at any one time, and the controls governing the use and storage of this material substantially reduce the hazard. In addition, the structure of the buildings and the type of manufacturing conducted classifies this facility as "general industrial occupancy" with the risk to life safety classified as low.

The implementation and enforcement of the fire protection plan will be primarily the responsibility of the (name) department, with secondary participation of the (name) and (name) departments.

Safety

Training

The safety department will initiate, through the individual manufacturing and support departments, employee training in incipient fire fighting. Each department supervisor will train employees by pointing out the location, type, and use of the fire extinguishers located in or available to that department. The supervisor will also show each new employee of his or her department the nearest fire exit and an alternate exit. This instruction will be reinforced monthly.

A specialty fire group will be formed and trained by the (name) department to evaluate and contain or extinguish any fire involving (area[s]/location[s]). This group will be made up of (names/titles).

Security

Fire alarm

A test of the fire alarm system at all facilities will be conducted each Monday morning at 8:00 A.M. The test will be conducted by (title) with notations made of the test results in the security daily log. Each test will be preceded by the announcement: "The fire alarm system is being tested. This is only a test." After the test is successfully concluded, another announcement will be made: "Attention. Testing of the fire alarm system has been completed. Respond to any further alarms."

Should the (name) fire department need to be called, it will be called by the senior security officer present and/or the senior manufacturing representative on duty during the second or third shift. During the first shift, the senior (title), (title), or (title) will make the decision to summon the fire department.

Fire drills

The safety department will conduct all fire drills at company facilities. The drills will generally be conducted twice a year, in October and April. Details will be provided prior to each drill.

Evacuation

The decision to evacuate this facility will be made by the appropriate fire department authorities or by management personnel in the order listed as follows:

A. (Title)
B. (Title)
C. (Title)
D. (Title)
E. (Title)

If evacuation is ordered by one of the individuals listed above, evacuees are to be assembled by department, in predetermined areas (see manufacturing below).

The security department will unlock or open all vehicle gates in the event the fire department is summoned.

Maintenance

Portable fire protection devices

It will be the responsibility of the (name) department to see that all portable fire protection devices are in a state of readiness at all times. Monthly inspection and reconditioning of all fire extinguishers will be conducted, unless more than five discharged extinguishers are available for recharging, at which time they will be recharged immediately.

The (name) department will be responsible for maintaining the self-contained breathing apparatus in a state of readiness at all times. They will also train appropriate personnel in the proper use of this apparatus initially and will reinforce this training with quarterly drills requiring all appropriate personnel to put on and test the equipment. A log will be kept indicating when each person completed the drill. The log will be audited periodically by the (title).

A visual inspection of all fire hydrants and post indicator valves (PIVs) will be conducted on a monthly basis, by the (name) department to insure they are all locked open. A log will be maintained in the (name) department with a copy sent each month to the (name) department.

All exterior fire and/or emergency exit routes will be maintained on a continuing basis to ensure a free and unobstructed flow of evacuating personnel.

The (name) department will be responsible for notifying the fire underwriting insurance company of all modifications to the sprinkler system or when a system is to be shut down regardless of duration. The names of individuals representing the insurance company will be provided to (department) by the (title).

All fire extinguishers will be appropriately numbered. A semiannual audit of fire extinguishers will be made jointly by the (name) and (name) departments.

Manufacturing (including support activities)

Training

Each department supervisor will be responsible for training his or her employees in the use and care of the portable fire protection devices available to that department. Supervisor training will be the responsibility of the (name) department.

Evacuation

An evacuation assembly area will be designated by each supervisor for his or her department. In the event an evacuation is necessary, the supervisor will make a head count of the department personnel and report the results to the security department or to the senior management person available. An evacuation order will be signaled by sounding the fire alarm and/or using the P.A. system.

Fire drills

Each supervisor will lead his or her personnel to the appropriate assembly point and conduct a head count.

The department supervisor will notify the (name) department of any discharged fire extinguishers.

In the event of a fire or any other emergency, the security department should be notified by dialing (number[s]).

Miscellaneous

The (title) will be notified immediately of any fire loss exceeding $1000; he or she, in turn, will so notify the (title).

The corporate (name) department will be notified immediately, through the office of the (title), of any fire resulting in losses of more than $1000. Notification will be made by (title).

All exterior and interior vehicle gates are to be physically identified. This facilitates fire department response to the closest area to the fire.

The (name) fire department should be familiarized with various gates and potential hazard areas. A semiannual meeting and tour should be scheduled to update fire department personnel about any changes or additions to the facilities or grounds.

A floor plan showing all emergency exits has been prepared and distributed to each department for posting. Each supervisor will note on this plan the primary and secondary fire exits to be used in the event of an evacuation.

A copy of this fire protection plan will be distributed to all supervisors.

A copy of this plan will be given to the (name) fire department. This plan will be updated by (title) as necessary to reflect any changes.

Evacuation Plan

In the event of any incident requiring evacuation of (company) facilities, the fire alarm will be sounded and/or an announcement made over the P.A. system advising personnel to evacuate.

Employees will assemble after evacuation at areas determined by the supervisors where a head count will be taken by the supervisor and reported to the security department or to the senior management person at the scene.

Once an employee has evacuated the facility, he or she is not to reenter *under any circumstances* unless so directed by supervision.

A site diagram showing evacuation routes, assembly points, and other control points has been distributed to all appropriate personnel. The (title) is responsible for maintaining this diagram in a current status.

ADP Protection Plan

(Place plan here.)

F

Bomb Threats
and Search Techniques

PURPOSE OF CALLS

The only two reasonable explanations for a call reporting that a bomb is to go off in a particular installation are:

1. The caller has definite knowledge or believes that an explosive or incendiary has been or will be placed and he wants to minimize personal injury or property damage. The caller may be the person who placed the device or someone else who has become aware of such information.
2. The caller wants to create an atmosphere of anxiety and panic which will, in turn, possibly result in a disruption of the normal activities at the installation where the device is purportedly located.

   When a bomb threat call has been received, there will be a reaction to it. If the call is directed to an installation where a vacuum of leadership exists or where there has been no organized advance planning to handle such threats, the call will result in panic.

Panic

Panic is one of the most contagious of all human emotions. Panic is defined as a "sudden, excessive, unreasoning, infectious terror." Panic is caused by fear—fear of the known or the unknown. Panic can also be defined in the context of a bomb threat call as the ultimate achievement of the caller.

Once a state of panic has been reached, the potential for personal injury and property damage is dramatically increased. Emergency and essential facilities can be shut down or abandoned and the community denied their use at a critical time.

Leaving facilities unattended can lead to destruction of the facility and the surrounding area. Large chemical manufacturing plants, power plants,

Courtesy of the Department of the Treasury, Bureau of Alcohol, Tobacco and Firearms (ATF P 7550.2 (4/75).

unattended boilers, and other such facilities require the attention of operating personnel.

Other effects of not being prepared or not having an organized plan to handle bomb threat calls can result in a lack of confidence in the leadership. This will be reflected in lower productivity or reluctance to continue employment at a location that is being subjected to bomb threat calls.

PREPARATION

Lines of organization and plans must be made in advance to handle bomb threats. Clear-cut levels of authority must be established. It is important that each person handle his assignment without delay and without any signs of fear.

Only by using an established organization and procedures can you handle these problems with the least risk. This will instill confidence and eliminate panic.

In planning, you should designate a control center or command post. This control center should be located in the switchboard room or other focal point of telephone or radio communications. The management personnel assigned to operate the control center should have decision-making authority on the action to be taken during the threat. Reports on the progress of the search and evacuation should be made to the control center. Only those with assigned duties should be permitted in the control center. Make some provision for alternates in the event someone is absent when the threat is received.

EVACUATION

The most serious of all decisions to be made by management in the event of a bomb threat is evacuation or nonevacuation of the building.

The decision to evacuate or not to evacuate may be made during the planning phase. Management may pronounce a carte blanche policy that in the event of a bomb threat, evacuation will be effected immediately. This decision circumvents the calculated risk and gives prime consideration for the safety of personnel in the building. This can result in production downtime, and can be costly, if the threat is a hoax. The alternative is for management to make the decision on the spot at the time of the threat. There is no magic formula which can produce the proper decision.

In the past, the vast majority of bomb threats turned out to be hoaxes. However, today more of the threats are materializing. Thus, management's first consideration must be for the safety of people. It is practically impossible to determine immediately whether a bomb threat is real.

Investigations have revealed that the targets for "terrorist bombings" are not selected at random. The modus operandi for selecting the target(s) and planting the explosive appears to follow this pattern. The target is selected because of political or personal gain to the terrorist. It is then kept under surveillance to determine the entrances and exits most used, and when. This is done to determine the hours when very few people are in the building. The idea is that the intent is not to injure or kill people, but to destroy the building. Reconnaissance of the building is made to locate an area where a bomb can be concealed, do the most damage, and where the "bomber" is least likely to be observed.

A test, or dry run, of the plan is often made. After the "dry run" and at a predetermined time, the building is infiltrated by the "bomber(s)" to deliver the explosives or incendiary device. The device may be fully or partially preset prior to planting. If it is fully set and charged, it is a simple matter for one or two of the group to plant the device in a preselected concealed area. This can be accomplished in a minimum of time. If the device is not fully set and charged, one member may act as a lookout while others arm and place the device. Most devices used for the destruction of property are usually of the time-delay type. These devices can be set for detonation to allow sufficient time for the "bomber(s)" to be a considerable distance away before the bomb-threat call is made and the device is detonated.

The terrorists have developed their plan of attack and the following procedures are suggested to business and industry for coping with bomb threats.

HOW TO PREPARE

1. Contact the police, fire department or other local governmental agencies to determine whether any has a bomb disposal unit. Under what conditions is the bomb disposal unit available? What is the telephone number? How can you obtain the services of the bomb disposal unit in the event of a bomb threat? Will the bomb disposal unit assist in the physical search of the building or will they only disarm or remove explosives?

2. Establish strict procedures for control and inspection of packages and material entering critical areas.

3. Develop a positive means of identifying and controlling personnel who are authorized access to critical areas.

4. Arrange, if possible, to have police and/or fire representatives with members of your staff inspect the building for areas where explosives are likely to be concealed. This may be accomplished by reviewing the floor plan of the building.

5. During the inspection of the building, you should give particular attention to elevator shafts, all ceiling areas, rest rooms, access doors, and crawl space in rest rooms and areas used as access to plumbing fixtures, electrical fixtures, utility and other closet areas, space under stairwells, boiler (furnace) rooms, flammable storage areas, main switches and valves, e.g., electric, gas, and fuel, indoor trash receptacles, record storage areas, mail rooms, ceiling lights with easily removable panels, and fire hose racks. While this list is not complete, it can give you an

idea where a time-delayed explosive or an incendiary device may be concealed.

6. All security and maintenance personnel should be alert to suspicious looking or unfamiliar persons or objects.

7. You should instruct security and maintenance personnel to make periodic checks of all rest rooms, stairwells, under stairwells, and other areas of the building to assure that unauthorized personnel are not hiding or reconnoitering or surveilling the area.

8. You should assure adequate protection for classified documents, proprietary information and other records essential to the operation of your business. A well-planted, properly charged device could, upon detonation, destroy those records needed in day-to-day operations. Computers have also been singled out as targets by bombers.

9. Instruct all personnel, especially those at the telephone switchboard, in what to do if a bomb threat call is received.

    As a minimum, every telephone operator or receptionist should be trained to respond calmly to a bomb threat call. To assist these individuals, a bomb threat call checklist of the type illustrated at the back of this appendix should be kept nearby. In addition, it is always desirable that more than one person listen in on the call. To do this, have a covert signalling system, perhaps a coded buzzer signal to a second reception point. A calm response to the bomb threat could result in getting additional information. This is especially true if the caller wishes to avoid injuries or deaths. If told that the building is occupied or cannot be evacuated in time, the bomber may be willing to give more specific information on the bomb's location.

10. Organize and train an evacuation unit consisting of key management personnel. The organization and training of this unit should be coordinated with other tenants of the building.

    a. The evacuation unit should be trained on how to evacuate the building during a bomb threat. You should consider priority of evacuation, that is, evacuation by floor level. Evacuate the floor levels above the danger area in order to remove those persons from danger as quickly as possible. Training in this type of evacuation should be available from police, fire or other units within the community.

    b. You may also train the evacuation unit in search techniques, or you may prefer a separate search unit. Volunteer personnel should be solicited for this function. Assignment of search wardens, team leaders, etc. can be employed. To be proficient in searching the building, search personnel must be thoroughly familiar with all hallways, restrooms, false ceiling areas and every location in the building where an explosive or incendiary device may be concealed. When the police or firemen arrive at the building, if they have not previously reconnoitered the building, the contents and

the floor plan will be strange to them. Thus, it is extremely important that the evacuation or search unit be thoroughly trained and
familiar with the floor plan of the building and immediate outside
areas. When the room or particular facility is searched it should be
marked or the room sealed with a piece of tape and reported to the
group supervisor.

c.   The evacuation or search unit should be trained only in evacuation
and search techniques and not in the techniques of neutralizing,
removing or otherwise having contact with the device. If a device
is located it should not be disturbed but a string or paper tape may
be run from the device location to a safe distance and used later
as a guide to the device.

When a Bomb Threat Is Called In

1.   Keep the caller on the line as long as possible. Ask him to repeat the
message. Record every word spoken by the person.
2.   If the caller does not indicate the location of the bomb or the time of possible detonation, you should ask him for this information.
3.   Inform the caller that the building is occupied and the detonation of a
bomb could result in death or serious injury to many innocent people.
4.   Pay particular attention to peculiar background noises such as, motors
running, background music, and any other noise which may give a clue
as to the location of the caller.
5.   Listen closely to the voice (male, female), voice quality (calm, excited),
accents and speech impediments. Immediately after the caller hangs up,
you should report to the person designated by management to receive
such information. Since the law enforcement personnel will want to talk
first-hand with the person who received the call, he should remain available until they appear.
6.   Report this information immediately to the police department, fire
department, ATF, FBI, and other appropriate agencies. The sequence of
notification should have been established during coordination in item
1 above.

WRITTEN THREATS

Save all materials, including any envelope or container. Once the message is
recognized as a bomb threat, further unnecessary handling should be avoided.
Every possible effort must be made to retain evidence such as fingerprints,
handwriting or typewriting, paper, and postal marks which are essential to
tracing the threat and identifying the writer.

While written messages are usually associated with generalized threats
and extortion attempts, a written warning of a specific device may occasion-
ally be received. It should never be ignored. With the growing use of voice
print identification techniques to identify and convict telephone callers,

there may well be an increase in the use of written warnings and calls to third parties.

BOMB SEARCH TECHNIQUES

1. Do not touch a strange or suspicious object. Its location and description should be reported to the person designated to receive this information.

2. The removal and disarming of a bomb or suspicious object must be left to the professionals in explosive ordnance disposal. Who these professionals are and how to contact them for assistance is something that you should include in any bomb threat plan.

3. All requests for assistance should be directed to one or more of the Emergency Numbers listed. Be sure that the telephone numbers for these agencies are included in your plan.

4. If the danger zone is located, the area should be blocked off or barricaded with a clear zone of three hundred feet until the object has been removed or disarmed.

5. During the search of the building, a rapid two-way communication system is of utmost importance. Such a system can be readily established through existing telephones. CAUTION—the use of radios during the search can be dangerous. The radio transmission energy can cause premature detonation of an electric initiator (blasting cap).

6. The signal for evacuating the building during a bomb threat should be the same as that used for evacuation in case of fire. The use of a different signal for bomb threats may create unnecessary excitement and confusion during evacuation.

7. If the building is evacuated, controls must be established immediately to prevent unauthorized access to the building. These controls may have to be provided by management. If proper coordination has been effected with the local police and other agencies, these may assist in establishing controls to prevent re-entry into the building until the danger has passed.

8. Evacuate the persons to a safe distance away from the building to protect them against debris and other flying objects if there is an explosion. If the building is evacuated, all gas and fuel lines should be cut off at the main valve. All electrical equipment should be turned off prior to evacuation. The decision to cut off all electrical power at the main switch should be made by management with consideration given to lighting requirements for search teams.

9. During the search, the medical personnel of the building should be alerted to stand by in case of an accident caused by an explosion of the device.

10. Fire brigade personnel should be alerted to stand by to man fire extinguishers.

11.   Pre-emergency plans should include a temporary relocation in the event the bomb threat materializes and the building is determined to be unsafe.

ROOM SEARCH

The following technique is based on use of a two-man searching team. There are many minor variations possible in searching a room. The following contains only the basic techniques.

First Team Action—listening

When the two-man search team enters the room to be searched, they should first move to various parts of the room and stand quietly, with their eyes shut and listen for a clock-work device. Frequently, a clock-work mechanism can be quickly detected without use of special equipment. Even if no clockwork mechanism is detected, the team is now aware of the background noise level within the room itself.

Background noise or transferred sound is always disturbing during a building search. In searching a building, if a ticking sound is heard but cannot be located, one might become unnerved. The ticking sound may come from an unbalanced air conditioner fan several floors away or from a dripping sink down the hall. Sound will transfer through air-conditioning ducts, along water pipes and through walls, etc. One of the worst types of buildings to work in is one that has steam or water heat. This type of building will constantly thump, crack, chatter and tick due to the movement of the steam or hot water through the pipes and the expansion and contraction of the pipes. Background noise may also be outside traffic sounds, rain, wind, etc.

Second Team Action—Division of Room and Selection of Search Height

The man in charge of the room searching team should look around the room and determine how the room is to be divided for searching and to what height the first searching sweep should extend. The first searching sweep will cover all items resting on the floor up to the selected height.

Dividing the Room

You should divide the room into two equal parts or as nearly equal as possible. This equal division should be based on the number and type of objects in the room to be searched, not the size of the room. An imaginary line is drawn between two objects in the room, that is, the edge of the window on the north wall to the floor lamp on the south wall.

Selection of First Searching Height

Look at the furniture or objects in the room and determine the average height of the majority of items resting on the floor. In an average room this height usually includes table or desk tops, chair backs, etc. The first searching height usually covers the items in the room up to hip height.

First Room Searching Sweep

After the room has been divided and a searching height has been selected, both men go to one end of the room division line and start from a back-to-back position. This is the starting point, and the same point will be used on each successive searching sweep. Each man now starts searching his way around the room, working toward the other man, checking all items resting on the floor around the wall area of the room. When the two men meet, they will have completed a "wall sweep" and should then work together and check all items in the middle of the room up to the selected hip height. Don't forget to check the floor under the rugs. This first searching sweep should also include those items which may be mounted on or in the walls, such as air-conditioning ducts, baseboard heaters, built-in wall cupboards, etc., if these fixtures are below hip height. The first searching sweep usually consumes the most time and effort. During all searching sweeps, use the electronic or medical stethescope on walls, furniture items, floors, etc.

Second Room Searching Sweep

The man in charge again looks at the furniture or objects in the room and determines the height of the second searching sweep. This height is usually from the hip to the chin or top of the head. The two men return to the starting point and repeat the searching techniques at the second selected searching height. This sweep usually covers pictures hanging on the walls, built-in book-cases, tall table lamps, etc.

Third Room Searching Sweep

When the second searching sweep is completed, the man in charge again determines the next searching height, usually from the chin or the top of the head up to the ceiling. The third sweep is then made. This sweep usually covers high mounted air-conditioning ducts, hanging light fixtures, etc.

Fourth Room Searching Sweep

If the room has a false or suspended ceiling, the fourth sweep involves investigation of this area. Check flush or ceiling-mounted light fixtures, air-conditioning or ventilation ducts, sound or speaker systems, electrical wiring, structural frame members, etc.

Have a sign or marker posted indicating "Search Completed" conspicuously in the area. Use a piece of colored scotch tape across the door and door jamb approximately two feet above floor level if the use of signs is not practical.

The room searching technique can be expanded. The same basic technique can be used to search a conventional hall or airport terminal.

Restated, to search an area you should:

1. Divide the area and select a search height
2. Start from the bottom and work up
3. Start back-to-back and work toward each other
4. Go around the walls then into the center of the room

Encourage the use of common sense or logic in searching. If a guest speaker at a convention has been threatened, common sense would indicate searching the speakers platform and microphones first, but always return to the searching technique. Do not rely on random or spot checking of only logical target areas. The bomber may not be a logical person.

(For comparison of seach systems, see the chart at the end of this appendix.)

SUSPICIOUS OBJECT LOCATED

Note: It is imperative that personnel involved in the search be instructed that their mission is only to search for and report suspicious objects, not to move, jar or touch the object or anything attached thereto. The removal/disarming of the bomb must be left to the professionals in explosive ordnance disposal. Remember that bombs and explosives are made to explode, and there are no absolutely safe methods of handling them.

1. Report the location and accurate description of the object to the appropriate warden. This information is relayed immediately to the control center who will call police, fire department, and rescue squad. These officers should be met and escorted to the scene.
2. Place sandbags or mattresses, not metal shield plates, around the object. Do not attempt to cover the object.
3. Identify the danger area, and block it off with a clear zone of at least 300 feet—include area below and above the object.
4. Check to see that all doors and windows are open to minimize primary damage from blast and secondary damage from fragmentation.
5. Evacuate the building.
6. Do not permit re-entry into the building until the device has been removed/disarmed, and the building declared safe for re-entry.

We in ATF recognize your responsibility to the public and the necessity for maintaining good public relations. This responsibility also includes the safety and protection of the public. We may well be approaching the point, when in the interest of security and protection of people, some inconvenience may have to be imposed on persons visiting public buildings.

Perhaps entrances and exits can be modified with a minimal expenditure to channel all personnel through someone at a registration desk. Personnel entering the building would be required to sign a register showing the name and room number of the person whom they wish to visit. Employees at these registration desks could contact the person to be visited and advise him that a visitor, by name, is in the lobby. The person to be visited may, in the interest of security and protection, decide to come to the lobby to meet this individual to ascertain that the purpose of the visit is valid and official. A system for signing out when the individual departs could be integrated into this procedure. There is no question that such a procedure would result in many complaints from the public. If it were explained to the visitor by the person at the registration desk that these procedures were implemented in his best interest and safety, the complaints would be reduced.

Other factors for consideration include:

1. Installation of closed-circuit television.
2. Installation of metal detecting devices.
3. Posting of signs indicating the use of closed circuit television or other detection devices.

The above are suggestions—in the final analysis of this entire complex problem, the decision is yours.

BUILDINGS—THEIR PROBLEM

The physical construction of buildings and their surrounding areas vary widely. Following are a few of the problems search teams will encounter.

Outside Areas

When you search outside areas, pay particular attention to street drainage systems, manholes in the street and in the sidewalk. Thoroughly check trash receptacles, garbage cans, dumpsters, incinerators, etc. Check parked cars and trucks. Check mail boxes if there is a history of placement in your area.

Schools

School bombings are usually directed against non-student areas. Find out which teachers or staff members are unpopular and where they work. The problem areas in schools are student lockers and the chemistry laboratory.

Student lockers are locked; no accurate record of the combinations are available because students change lockers at will. Every other locker seems to "tick." Alarm clocks, wrist watches, leaking thermos jugs and white mice, all make "ticking" sounds. Have the school authorities or police cut off the locks; then search teams should open the lockers. If you cut off the lock you may end up paying for it.

Chemistry labs should be treated with caution. Each year some student tries to make an explosive mixture or rocket fuel in the classroom, gets scared, and phones in a bomb call. The best procedure is to get the chemistry teacher and ask him to inspect the classroom, lab and chemical storage area with you. He will know 90% of the items in the lab which leaves only 10% to worry about.

If repeated bomb threats are received at schools in your area, recommend that the school board hold make-up classes on Saturday. This tends to cut down the number of bomb scares.

Office Buildings

The biggest problem in office buildings is many locked desks. A repair of desk locks is an expensive item. There will be many other items to keep you busy, such as filing cabinets, storage closets, wall lockers, etc. Watch out for the company's security system if they deal in fashions of any type, the automotive or aircraft industry, defense contracts, or the toy industry. Electrical leads, electrical tapes, electrical eyes, electrical pressure mats, electrical microswitches, will all ring those huge bells that no one knows how to turn off.

Auditoriums, Amphitheaters, and Convention Halls

Here, thousands of seats must be checked on hands and knees. Look for cut or unfastened seats with a bomb inserted into the cushion or back. Check out the stage area which has tons of equipment in it; also the speaker's platform and the microphones. The area under the stage generally has crawlways, tunnels, trapdoors, dressing rooms, and storage areas. The sound system is extensive and the air-conditioning system is unbelievable. The entire roof area, in a theater, frequently has one huge storage room and maintenance area above it. Check all hanging decorations and lighting fixtures.

Airport Terminals

This structure combines all problems covered under schools, office buildings, and auditoriums, plus outside areas and aircraft.

AIRCRAFT

The complexities of aircraft design make it unlikely that even the trained searcher will locate any but the most obvious explosive or incendiary device. Thus, detailed searches of large aircraft must be conducted by maintenance and crew personnel who are entirely familiar with the construction and equipment of the plane. In emergency situations where searches must be conducted by public safety personnel without the aid of aircraft specialists, the following general procedures should be used:

1. Evacuate the area and remove all personal property.
2. Check the area around the craft for bombs, wires or evidence of tampering.
3. Tow the aircraft to a distant area.
4. Starting on the outside, work toward the plane's interior.
5. Begin searching at the lowest level and work up.
6. Remove freight and baggage and search cargo areas.

7. Check out rest rooms and lounges.
8. Be alert for small charges placed to rupture the pressure hull or cut control cables. The control cables usually run underneath the center aisle.
9. With special attention to refuse disposal containers, check food preparation and service areas.
10. Search large cabin areas in two sweeps.
11. Check the flight deck.
12. Simultaneously, search the baggage and freight in a safe area under the supervision of airline personnel. If passengers are asked to come forward to identify and open their baggage for inspection, it may be possible to quickly focus in upon unclaimed baggage.

Elevator Wells and Shafts

Elevator wells are usually one to three feet deep with grease, dirt and trash and must be probed by hand. To check elevator shafts, get on the top of the car with two six-volt lanterns, move the car up a floor (or part of a floor) at a time and look around the shaft. Be prepared to find nooks, closets, storage rooms, false panels, walk areas, and hundreds of empty whiskey bottles in paper bags. Don't forget that as you go up, the counterweights are coming down—check them too. The elevator machinery is generally located on the roof. A Word of Caution: Watch for strong winds in the elevator shaft. Don't stand near the edge of the car.

Handling of the News Media

It is of paramount importance that all inquiries by the news media be directed to one person appointed as spokesman. All other persons should be instructed not to discuss the situation with outsiders, especially the news media.

The purpose of this provision is to furnish the news media with accurate information and see that additional bomb threat calls are not precipitated by irresponsible statements from uninformed sources.

ADDITIONAL INFORMATION

Both government and private sources have aids dealing with bomb threats and bombings. Among those available on request from the Bureau of Alcohol, Tobacco and Firearms, Washington, D.C. 20226 are the following:

1. A pamphlet explaining Title XI of the Omnibus Crime Control and Safe Streets Act
2. A booklet of Questions and Answers on Federal Law concerning explosives under Title XI
3. A reprint of Title XI of the Law

"Property Protection During Civil Disturbances" is available from Factory Insurance Association, 85 Woodland St., Hartford, Connecticut 06102.

The publishing house of Charles C. Thomas, 301 East Lawrence Ave., Springfield, Illinois 62717, has four books on the subject: "Explosives and Homemade Bombs" by Stoffel; "Bombs and Bombings" by Tom G. Brodie; "Explosives and Bomb Disposal Guide" by Lenz; and "Protection Against Bombs and Incendiaries" by Pike.

Three films entitled "Bombs I, II and III" are available from Motorola Teleprograms, Inc., Suite 26, 4825 N. Scott St., Schiller Park, Illinois 60176, ATTN: Mr. Lloyd Singer, President. These are on 16 mm, Super 8 mm, Videotape and Videocassettes. They also have a workbook on bomb scare planning and conduct seminars. Mail your request for information on a company letterhead.

William Brose Productions Inc., 3168 Oakshire Drive, Hollywood, California 90068, has two films: "Bomb Threat! Plan Don't Panic" (15 min.); and "High-fire! Plan for Survival" (19 min.). The last deals with evacuating high rise office buildings.

LETTER AND PACKAGE BOMBS

Background

Letter and package bombs are not new. While the latest incidents have involved political terrorism, such bombs are made for a wide variety of motives. The particular form of these bombs varies in size, shape and components. They may have electric, nonelectric or other sophisticated firing systems.

Precautions

Mail handlers should be alert to recognize suspicious looking items. Mail should be separated into "personal" and "business." Although there is no approved, standard detection method, the following precautions are suggested:

1. Look at the sender's address. Is it a familiar one?
2. Is correspondence from the sender expected?
    Do the characteristics of the envelope or package resemble the expected contents?
3. If the item is from another country, ask yourself if it is expected. Do you have relatives or friends traveling? Did you buy something from business associates, charitable or religious groups, international organizations, etc.?

If you have a suspicious looking letter or package:
  Do not try to open it.
  Isolate it and evacuate everyone in the vicinity to a safe distance.
  Notify local police and await their arrival.

Suggested form to be completed by investigators following

BOMB THREAT CALLS

Type of Complainant:

☐ School   ☐ Hospital   ☐ Industrial Manufacturing Company
☐ Business   ☐ Other

Business Name of Complainant

Business Address

Business Telephone

Name of Person Reporting Complaint

Telephone Number That Call Was Received On   Date and Time of Call

Name of Person Who Talked to the Caller

Exact Words said by Caller

Background Noises (i.e., Street Sounds, Baby Crying, etc.)

Information about Caller:

Age	Sex	Race	Accent	Educational Level

Speech Impediments (Drunk, Lisp, etc.)   Attitude (Calm, Excited, etc.)

Any Suspects?
☐ Yes   ☐ No

Have Previous Calls Been Received?
☐ Yes   ☐ No   If Yes, Approximately How Many?

Has the Telephone Company Security Department Been Notified?
☐ Yes   ☐ No

Was any Incendiary or Explosive Device Found?
☐ Yes   ☐ No

Number of Threats Received Thus Far During Calendar Year

CHECK LIST WHEN YOU RECEIVE A BOMB THREAT

Time and Date Reported: _____

How Reported: _____

Exact Words of Caller: _____

_____

_____

Questions to Ask: _____

1. When is bomb going to explode? _____

2. Where is bomb right now? _____

3. What kind of bomb is it? _____

4. What does it look like? _____

5. Why did you place the bomb? _____

6. Where are you calling from? _____

Description of Caller's Voice: _____

Male ____ Female ____ Young ____ Middle Age ____ Old ____ Accent ____

Tone of Voice _____ Background Noise _____ Is voice familiar? _____

If so, who did it sound like? _____

_____

Other voice characteristics: _____

Time Caller Hung Up: _____ Remarks: _____

_____

_____

_____

Name, Address, Telephone of Recipient: _____

_____

_____

RECORD:

1. Date _____ and time _____ of call.

2. Exact language used. _____

_____

_____

_____

_____

_____

_____

3. ☐ Male   ☐ Female
    ☐ Adult   ☐ Child

Estimated age _____ Race _____

4. Speech (Check applicable boxes)

   ☐ Slow   ☐ Excited   ☐ Disguised
   ☐ Rapid   ☐ Loud   ☐ Broken
   ☐ Normal   ☐ Normal   ☐ Sincere

   Accent _____

5. Background noises _____

_____

_____

_____

_____

6. Name of person receiving the call

SEARCH SYSTEMS

	ADVANTAGES	DISADVANTAGES	THOROUGHNESS
S U P E R V I S O R Y — SEARCH BY: Supervisors	BEST for Covert search POOR for thoroughness POOR for morale if detected 1. Covert 2. Fairly rapid 3. Loss of working time of supervisor only	1. Unfamiliarity with many areas 2. Will not look in dirty places 3. Covert search is difficult to maintain 4. Generally results in search of obvious areas, *not* hard-to-reach ones 5. Violation of privacy problems 6. Danger to unevacuated workers	50–65%
O C C U P A N T — SEARCH BY: Occupants	BEST for speed of search GOOD for thoroughness GOOD for morale (with confidence in training given beforehand) 1. Rapid 2. No privacy violation problem 3. Loss of work time for shorter period of time than for evacuation 4. Personal concern for own safety leads to good search 5. Personnel conducting search are familiar with area	1. Requires training of entire work force 2. Requires several practical training exercises 3. Danger to unevacuated workers	80–90%
T E A M — SEARCH BY: Trained Team	BEST for safety BEST For thoroughness BEST for morale POOR for lost work time 1. Thorough 2. No danger to workers who have been evacuated 3. Workers feel company cares for their safety	1. Loss of production time 2. Very slow operation 3. Requires comprehensive training and practice 4. Privacy violation problems	90–100%

☆ *U.S. Government Printing Office: 1975#629-411/198-31*

G

Federal Emergency Management Agency (FEMA) Publications

The following is a partial listing of the publications available from the Federal Emergency Management Agency (FEMA). General information on FEMA publications is available at the end of this list.

CPG 1–3
Federal Assistance Handbook: Emergency Management, Direction and Control Programs

This handbook is designed to help state and local governments take advantage of selected assistance provided under the Federal Civil Defense Act of 1950, as amended, in order to develop, maintain, and improve their emergency operating capabilities. This handbook includes definitions, descriptions, standards, and procedures.

CPG 1–5
Objectives for Local Emergency Management

The purpose of this guide is to assist local Emergency Program Managers and their staffs in developing and maintaining a comprehensive and integrated emergency management program. The objectives set forth suggest actions local governments should undertake in relation to the specific hazards that potentially face their jurisdictions. They indicate what activities should be pursued but do not provide the specifics on how to accomplish them. Guidance for developing particular functions or programs is contained in other FEMA publications referenced in the Table of Contents.

CPG 1–6
Disaster Operations—A Handbook for Local Governments

A planning and operations guide for local government officials in small municipalities and counties. Includes checklist pertaining to a number of specific types of civil emergencies that could confront such communities.

CPG 1–7
Guide for Increasing Local Government Civil Defense Readiness During Periods of International Crisis

This guide has 21 sections concerned with actions to increase readiness during an international crisis in areas including emergency public information, direction and control, shelter and others.

CPG 1–8
Local Government Emergency Planning

This guide covers planning for emergencies or disasters.

CPG 1–17
Outdoor Warning Systems Guide

This guide has been developed to aid public officials in determining the requirements for outdoor warning systems.

CPG 1–18
Emergency Communications

Prescribes procedures for the development of detailed plans for the effective use of existing communications resources during an emergency.

CPG 1–20
Emergency Operating Centers Handbook

This handbook is designed to provide information to State and local officials responsible for emergency management on the need for and the development of a direction and control capacity in their communities.

CPG 2–5
Disaster Planning Guide for Business and Industry

Coordinated planning with your local civil preparedness director should assure provisions for the fullest use of community resources as needed. Mutual assistance agreements with other industrial facilities provide insurance for use in emergencies. This publication gives the basic keys for developing plans for industry and business in the event of a disaster.

CPG 2–13
Guidelines for Maintenance of Emergency Use Equipment

This guideline describes the preventive maintenance program and reporting systems developed for emergency equipment not in everyday use. Information is provided about contract provisions where such maintenance should normally be done by contract. Detailed examples of standard maintenance guides are provided to assist state and local governments in establishing their programs.

CPG 2–15
Transportation Planning Guidelines for the Evacuation of Large Populations

These guidelines have been developed to assist population protection planners throughout the U.S. with the task of developing transportation plans for the large-scale evacuation of major population centers. These guidelines review past research, present a basic framework of essential planning elements, present techniques for assigning vehicle routing and illustrates planning techniques with examples.

CPG 2–16
A Guide to Hurricane Preparedness Planning for State and Local Officials
This guide has been prepared to assist State and local officials in the development of emergency management capabilities which provide confidence that the jurisdiction can deal effectively with the unique characteristics of the hurricane hazards. It provides guidance on the conduct of a Quantitative Hurricane Preparedness Study which includes the organization, management, coordination system, planning methodology, and general information concerning objectives, funding, government roles, program maintenance, and evaluation.

CPG 2–1A Series: Attack Environment Manuals have been prepared to help the emergency planner understand what nuclear war may be like, and summarizes what FEMA knows about nuclear attack environment as it may affect operational readiness at local levels. The following chapters, published separately, have been issued to date.

CPG 2–1A1
FEMA Attack Environment Manual
Chapter 1—Introduction to Nuclear Emergency Operations

CPG 2–1A2
FEMA Attack Environment Manual
Chapter 2—What the Planner Needs to Know About Blast and Shock

CPG 2–1A3
FEMA Attack Environment Manual
Chapter 3—What the Planner Needs to Know About Fire Ignition and Spread

CPG 2–1A4
FEMA Attack Environment Manual
Chapter 4—What the Planner Needs to Know About Electromagnetic Pulse

CPG 2–1A5
FEMA Attack Environment Manual
Chapter 5–What the Planner Needs to Know About Initial Nuclear Radiation

CPG 2–1A6
FEMA Attack Environment Manual
Chapter 6—What the Planner Needs to Know About Fallout

CPG 2–1A7
FEMA Attack Environment Manual
Chapter 7—What the Planner Needs to Know About the Shelter Environment

CPG 2–1A8
FEMA Attack Environment Manual
Chapter 8—What the Planner Needs to Know About the Post-Shelter Environment

CPG 2–1A9
FEMA Attack Environment Manual
Chapter 9—Application to Emergency Operations Planning

CPC 83–1
Shelter Supplies
The purpose of this circular is to provide the most recent information on the condition of shelter supplies to assist local governments in making decisions on the use of and disposition of the supplies. In addition, this circular is being issued to emphasize the possible hazards of distributing such goods and the local authorities responsibility to assure the safety of these products prior to disposition.

CPC 84–2
A Conceptual Approach to State and Local Exercises
This circular reviews the importance of exercises to state and local preparedness, examines some of the problems associated with exercises, presents some suggestions for resolving these problems, and suggests an approach to the design, conduct, and evaluation of a practical exercise program for state and local use.

TR–20
Vol. III
Shelter Environmental Support Systems, Volume III
In this revision the environmental support systems are oriented specifically for Emergency Operating Centers (EOC's) from which key government and emergency services officials can direct activities essen-

tial to saving lives and safeguarding property.

TR-62
Increasing Blast and Fire Resistance in Buildings
This booklet reviews briefly the environment created by nuclear explosions, the potential hazards, and the response of buildings and their inhabitants to the environment. Also provides basic concepts of design techniques for increasing protection against blast and fire effects in buildings.

TR–73
ENVIRONMENT: Problems, Solutions, and Emergency Preparedness
This report shows how architects and engineers can meet the challenge of the many present day dangers through the total design concepts.

TR–83A
Interim Guidelines for Building Occupant Protection from Tornadoes and Extreme Winds
Provides guidelines for use by Architects and Engineers in designing and building-in protection from high winds generated by tornadoes and other severe storms.

TR–83B
Tornado Protection—Selecting and Designing Safe Areas in Buildings
Provides information of interest to building owners, hospital and school administrators, and architects and engineers. Contains guidance on reviewing a building and determining the location of the safest area.

H–15
Basic Course in Emergency Mass Feeding
Handbook developed jointly by the Department of Defense, Defense Civil Preparedness Agency (now FEMA), the American National Red Cross, and the Welfare Administration—Department of Health, Education, and Welfare (now the Department of Health and Human Services), for use primarily by students taking the basic course. May also serve as a ready reference for food workers engaged in actual emergency feeding operations.

TM 75–1
Converting Vehicles for Use as Fire Apparatus or Rescue Trucks
Provides information on how a local government can convert vehicles obtained through the FEMA surplus or contributions loan programs into fire apparatus or rescue trucks.

P&P–10
A Climatological Oil Spill Planning Guide Number 2
This study is to provide such information in a format that can be understood and used in oil spill contingency planning and by scientific support personnel during actual spills.

DR&R–1
Handbook for Applicants
This handbook prescribes policy and procedures for requesting, obtaining and administering FEMA grants for public assistance under the Disaster Relief Act of 1974 (P.L. 93–288).

DR&R–2
Eligibility Handbook
A handbook for determining eligible applicants for public assistance and categories of eligible work under the Disaster Relief Act of 1974 (P.L. 93–288).

DR&R–3
Insurance Handbook for Public Assistance
A policy and procedural handbook for local, state and federal officials concerned with administering general hazard insurance and flood insurance requirements under the Disaster Relief Act of 1974 (P.L. 93–288).

DR&R–4
Fire Suppression Assistance Handbook
A handbook for state and federal officials in the administration of fire suppression assistance under the Disaster Relief Act of 1974 (P.L. 93–288).

DR&R–5
Community Disaster Loan Handbook
A handbook for local governments and state and federal officials outlining the Community Disaster Loan program under the Disaster Relief Act of 1974 (P.L. 93–288). Provides information concerning eligibility, application, administration and settlement.

DR&R–6
Federal Disaster Assistance Program Environmental Review Handbook
This handbook sets forth FEMA policies, procedures and assignment

of responsibilities for the implementation of the National Environmental Policy Act of 1969, (NEPA), Public Law 91–190, pursuant to the Disaster Relief Act of 1974 (P.L. 93–288).

DR&R–7
Documenting Disaster Damage

This handbook is concerned with the need to maintain proper records so that you can fill out, update, maintain and submit various papers, in order to receive Federal Emergency Management Agency funds.

DR&R–10
Your Disaster Assistance Center: Federal, State and Local Aid

Handbook on how to apply for assistance after a disaster.

DR&R–16
When You Return to a Storm-Damaged Home

A handbook providing general instructions for entering and prompt clean-up of disaster-damaged building.

DR&R–19
PROGRAM GUIDE: Disaster Assistance Programs

This handbook is issued by the Office of Disaster Assistance Programs, State and Local Programs and Support, as a general overview of supplemental federal disaster assistance. This handbook describes the declaration process for presidentially declared major disasters and emergencies. It details the assistance available under Public Law 93–288, the Disaster Relief Act of

1974, and related authorities under other federal assistance programs. A listing is also included for FEMA regional offices and corresponding emergency offices in each state.

IG 8
Basic Rescue Course

This publication contains the first steps in developing standard procedures for rescue from damaged buildings, and techniques on removing survivors and safety measures.

IG 9
Light Duty Rescue Course

Provides training for individuals who will become members of organized rescue squads for releasing injured and uninjured people trapped in lightly damaged structures or in shelters with limited access problems.

IG 110
Analysis of Hazardous Materials Emergencies for Emergency Program Managers

The course assists local emergency program managers and emergency response personnel to define the problem posed by hazardous materials in an emergency. Additionally, the technical aspects and management issues that surround hazardous materials emergencies are addressed.

IG 132
Basic Disaster Operations Course

Designed to introduce the state and local emergency managers to basic concepts and operations of a disaster assistance environment, especially in terms of major disaster incidents, and to enhance understanding of state and local roles in the overall recovery effort. Student Materials are contained in the Instructor Guide.

SM 2
Law and Order Training for Civil Defense Emergency—Student Manual Part A

This manual was designed primarily for training auxiliary police for civil defense emergencies. Police training should be carried out by the police chief or sheriff.

SM 11
How to Manage Congregate Lodging Facilities and Fallout Shelters

This manual is an easy to follow series of instructions to guide an individual through the things that need to be done and the problems that may have to be solved, while managing a congregate care or fallout shelters.

SM 20
Communication Skills for Disaster Workers

Motivations and expectations of disaster workers working in a disaster response and recovery environment is a demanding job, both physically and emotionally. The purpose of manual section is to help you explore some of your own attitudes and feelings about the work, so you will be better prepared for dealing with the tensions you will undoubtedly experience.

SM 21
Public Affairs Workshop

Manual was developed to train individuals to work with the media, editorial, audiovisual, manage news conferences and awareness projects.

SM 51
Formulating Public Policy in Emergency Management

This publication focuses on the public official's role in establishing public policy in emergency management and executing public policy during high-stress emergencies.

SM 60
Introduction to Emergency Management

This publication is intended to provide orientation to the emergency management field: to offer information that will enable the newcomer to develop a clearer view of the generic emergency management system and to offer assistance in clarifying the nature of roles in that system. The primary purpose of the course is to enable you to find a route that can make you as productive and harmonious a member of the emergency protection team as your position warrants.

SM 61
Emergency Planning

The goal of this course is to develop your skills and to increase your understanding of the procedures and processes required to create an effective emergency management plan. To achieve this, the course will provide 5 days of training covering three sections.

SM 170.1
Exercise Design Course

This manual contains forms, checklists and sample documents which would be used by exercise design course participants. Used in conjunction with SM 170.2.

SM 170.2
Exercise Design Course—Guide to Emergency Management Exercise

This is the primary text for the exercise design course. Its primary purpose is to help state and local governments design, prepare, conduct, and evaluate exercises.

SM 170.3
Exercise Design Course—Exercise Scenarios

This manual is optional student material for the exercise design course. It contains sample exercise scenarios for a variety of natural and manmade hazards.

SS-1
Emergency Program Manager: An Orientation to the Position

Self-study for new Emergency Program Managers. Course covers: Comprehensive Emergency Management, Roles and Responsibilities of Emergency Program Managers, Mitigation, Preparedness, Response, Recovery and Managing Emergency Management.

SS-2
Emergency Management, U.S.A.

Self-study course for the average U.S. citizen based on the comprehensive emergency management approach. Describes natural and technological hazards and the nuclear attack threat. Leads the citizens through the developing personal emergency prepareness plans and encourages participation in the emergency network.

TD-8
Industrial Protection Guide

This publication contains ten sections, which is a plan to save lives and resources in case of nuclear disaster or other emergencies.

FEMA-10
Planning Guide and Checklist for Hazardous Materials Contingency Plans

This publication is designed to assist state and local officials develop a plan to respond to hazardous chemical spills from the smallest to the most complex.

FEMA-46
Earthquake Safety Checklist

Safety tips for preparation, response to, and immediate aftermath of an earthquake.

FEMA-47
Family Earthquake Drill

Steps to follow in the event of a major earthquake. Designed for family discussion.

FEMA-48
Coping with Children's Reactions to Earthquakes and Other Disasters

This publication deals with Children's fears and anxieties following a disaster.

FEMA–50
Preparing for Hurricanes and Coastal Flooding

This publication focuses on two of the most common coastal hazards: tidal flooding and hurricanes. It is designed to help communities prepare for these common coastal hazards.

FEMA–59
Shelter Management Handbook

This handbook provides the step-by-step instructions for effective shelter operations, such as organizations, operational procedures shelter operations, etc.

GENERAL INFORMATION ON FEMA PUBLICATIONS

Availability of Publications

Publications and other printed matter produced by FEMA are available, upon request, subject to availability of stock.

How to Obtain Publications

- State and local Emergency Management offices may obtain additional quantities from the FEMA Regional Offices (or from FEMA, P.O. Box 8181, Washington, D.C. 20024 in accordance with established regional procedures.
- FEMA activities (Headquarters & Regional) may obtain quantities of publications by submitting FEMA Form 60–8, Requisition for Publications and Blank Forms to FEMA, P.O. Box 8181, Washington, D.C. 20024.
- FEMA Headquarters requirements for single copies of publications may be obtained by submitting FEMA Form 60–8, Requisition for Publications and Blank Forms to the Printing and Publications Division, Room 324.

How to Obtain Emergency Management Training and Education Publications

State and local Emergency Management offices and other training institutions may obtain additional training publications by completing FEMA Form 60–8 and submitting it to the appropriate State Emergency Management Office. After reviewing, they will forward it to the appropriate FEMA Regional Office, attn: T&E Program Manager for approval. All requests for training materials *must* receive Regional Training approval.

It should also be noted that training publications are only available for the purpose of supporting field training courses. Approval for all other requests will be based on the justification listed on the Publications Form.

Prescribed Form

This publication prescribes the use of FEMA Form 60–8, Requisition for Publications and Blank Forms, which may be obtained from Printing and Publications Division, Office of Administrative Support or FEMA, P.O. Box 8181, Washington, D.C. 20024.

Identification of Publications

- All requests should include the reference (identification number) and the full title of each publication.
- Include your full address and zip code.

FEMA REGIONAL OFFICES

Address	States Serviced
FEMA Region I 442 J.W. McCormack, POCH Boston, MA 02109	Connecticut, Maine, Vermont, Massachusetts, New Hampshire, Rhode Island
FEMA Region II 26 Federal Plaza, RM 1349 New York, NY 10278	New York, New Jersey, Puerto Rico, Virgin Islands
FEMA Region III 105 S. Seventh Street, 2nd Floor Philadelphia, PA 19106	Delaware, Maryland, Virginia, Pennsylvania, District of Columbia, West Virginia
FEMA Region IV Suite 700 1371 Peachtree Street, NE Atlanta, GA 30309	Alabama, Georgia, Florida, Mississippi, Kentucky, South Carolina, North Carolina, Tennessee
FEMA Region V 300 South Wacker Drive Chicago, IL 60606	Indiana, Illinois, Wisconsin, Ohio, Minnesota, Michigan
FEMA Region VI Federal Regional Center 800 N. Loop 288, Rm 206 Denton, TX 76201	Arkansas, Louisiana, Texas, New Mexico, Oklahoma
FEMA Region VII 911 Walnut Street, Rm 300 Kansas City, MO 64106	Kansas, Nebraska, Missouri, Iowa
FEMA Region VIII Denver Federal Center Building 710, Box 25267 Denver, CO 80225–0267	Colorado, Montana, Utah, North Dakota, South Dakota, Wyoming

FEMA Region IX
Building 105
Presidio of San Francisco,
  CA 94129

California, Arizona, Nevada,
Hawaii, Pacific Commonwealths
and Territories

FEMA Region X
Federal Regional Center
130 228th Street, S.W.
Bothell, WA 98021–9796

Idaho, Oregon, Washington,
Alaska

Index